The Prince of of Dav

J. H. Ingraham

Alpha Editions

This edition published in 2024

ISBN 9789362097224

Design and Setting By

Alpha Editions

www.alphaedis.com

Email - info@alphaedis.com

Contents

PREFACE.   - 1 -

LETTER I.   - 2 -

LETTER II.   - 5 -

LETTER III.   - 9 -

LETTER IV.   - 13 -

LETTER V.   - 18 -

LETTER VI.   - 27 -

LETTER VII.   - 31 -

LETTER VIII.   - 34 -

LETTER IX.   - 38 -

LETTER X.   - 43 -

LETTER XI.   - 46 -

LETTER XII.   - 51 -

LETTER XIII.   - 55 -

LETTER XIV.   - 59 -

LETTER XV.   - 62 -

LETTER XVI.   - 66 -

LETTER XVII.   - 71 -

LETTER XVIII.   - 76 -

LETTER XIX.   - 81 -

LETTER XX.   - 85 -

LETTER XXI.   - 89 -

LETTER XXII.   - 94 -

LETTER XXIII.   - 100 -

LETTER XXIV.   - 103 -

LETTER XXV.   - 107 -

LETTER XXVI.   - 109 -

LETTER XXVII.   - 114 -

LETTER XXVIII.   - 121 -

LETTER XXIX.   - 125 -

LETTER XXX.   - 135 -

LETTER XXXI.   - 140 -

LETTER XXXII.   - 148 -

LETTER XXXIII.   - 156 -

LETTER XXXIV.   - 162 -

LETTER XXXV.   - 169 -

LETTER XXXVI.   - 177 -

LETTER XXXVII.   - 182 -

LETTER XXXVIII.   - 188 -

LETTER XXXIX.   - 192 -

PREFACE.

The "Prince of the House of David," written by Rev. Mr. Ingraham, needs no recommendation. Its fame has been, long since, established, and its fascination has already held sway over multitudes of delighted readers. Recognizing fully its merits, the publishers of this edition decided to put it in the way of a still greater circulation; and in order to facilitate this, it has been thoroughly revised and in parts re-written, all unnecessary repetition appearing in the original edition of the book being omitted.

Adina, the suppositious writer of the following letters, is the daughter of a Jew who resides in Alexandria, Egypt. She has come to Jerusalem during the most stirring period of earth's history, and, from thence, for the period of three years, she keeps her father apprized of the marvelous events occurring about her during that time.

THE PUBLISHERS.

LETTER I.

My Dear Father:

My first duty, as it is my highest pleasure, is to comply with your command to write you as soon as I should arrive at Jerusalem, and this letter, while it conveys intelligence of my arrival, will confirm to you my filial obedience.

My journey hither occupied many days. When we traveled in sight of the sea, which we did for three days, I enjoyed the majesty of the prospect, it seemed so like the sky stretched out upon the earth. I also had the good fortune to see several ships, which the Rabbi informed me were Roman galleys, bound some to Sidon, and others into the Nile; and after one of these latter, as it was going to you, I sent a prayer and a wish. Just as we were leaving the sea-shore to turn off into the desert, I saw a wrecked vessel. It looked so helpless and bulky, with its huge black body all out of the water, that it seemed to me like a great sea-monster, stranded and dying; and I felt like pitying it. How terrible a tempest must be upon the sea! I was in hopes to have seen a Leviathan, but was not gratified in the wish. The good Rabbi, who seemed to know all about these things, told me that they seldom appear now in the Middle Sea, but are seen beyond the pillar of Hercules at the world's end.

At Gaza we stopped two days, and from thence we proceeded over-land to our destination.

The morning of the last day of our journey but one, having lost our way and wandered many hours eastwardly, we caught sight of the Sea of Sodom and Gomorrah, at a great distance to the east. How my pulse quickened at beholding that fearful spot! I seemed to see in imagination the heavens on fire above it, and the flames and smoke ascending as from a great furnace, as on that fearful day when they were destroyed, with all that beautiful surrounding plain, which we are told was one vast garden of beauty. How calm and still lay now that sluggish sea beneath a cloudless sky! We held it in sight many hours, and once caught a glimpse of the Jordan north of it, looking like a silver thread; yet near as it appeared to be, I was told it was a good day's journey for a camel to reach its shores.

After losing sight of this melancholy lake, our way lay along a narrow valley for some time, and the next day, on reaching an eminence, Jerusalem appeared, as if risen out of the earth.

I cannot, my dear father, describe to you my emotions on beholding the Holy City! They have been experienced by millions of our people—they were similar to your own as you related them to me. All the past, with its mighty men who walked with Jehovah, rushed to my memory, and compelled me to bow my head, and worship and adore at the sight of the Temple, where God once (alas, why does he no longer visit earth and his holy house?) dwelt in the flaming Shechinah, and made known the oracles of his will.

We entered the city just before the sixth hour of the evening, and were soon at the house of our relative, Amos, the Levite. I was received as if I had a daughter's claim to their embraces; and with the luxuries with which they surrounded me in my gorgeously furnished apartments. I am sure my kinsfolk here mean to tempt me to forget the joys of the dear home I have left.

The Rabbi Amos and his family all desire to be commended to you. He seems to be a man of piety and benevolence, and greatly loves his children. I have been once to the Temple. Its outer court seemed like a vast caravanserai or market-place, being thronged with the men who sell animals for sacrifice, which crowded all parts. Thousands of doves in large cages were sold on one side, and on another were stalls for lambs, sheep, calves and oxen, the noise and bleating of which, with the confusion of tongues, made the place appear like anything else than the Temple of Jehovah. It appears like desecration to use the Temple thus, dear father, and seems to show a want of that holy love of God's house that once characterized our ancestors. On reaching the women's court I was sensible of being in the Temple, by the magnificence which surrounded me. With what awe I bowed my head in the direction of the Holy of Holies! I never felt before so near to God! Clouds of incense floated above the heads of the multitude, and rivers of blood flowed down the marble steps of the altar of burnt offering. Alas! how many innocent victims bleed every morning and evening for the sins of Israel! What a sea of blood has been poured out in ages that have passed! What a strange, fearful mystery, that the blood of an innocent lamb should atone for sins I have done! There must be some deeper meaning in these sacrifices, dear father, yet unrevealed to us.

As I was returning from the Temple I met many persons, who seemed to be crowding out of the gate on some unusual errand. I have since learned that they were going to see a very extraordinary man—a true prophet of God, it is believed by many, who dwells in the wilderness eastward near Jordan, and who preaches with power unknown in the land since the days of Elijah and Elisha. I hope he is a true prophet of heaven, and that God is once more about to remember Israel, but the days of the Prophets have long passed away, and I fear this man is only an enthusiast.

Farewell, dear father, and let us ever pray for the glory of Israel.

Your affectionate,

Adina.

LETTER II.

My Dear Father:

The street in which we dwell is elevated, and from the roof of the house, where I love to walk in the evening, watching the stars that hang over Egypt, there is commanded a wide prospect of the Holy City.

Yesterday morning I was early on the house-top, to behold the first cloud of the day-dawn sacrifice rise from the bosom of the Temple. When I had turned my gaze towards the sacred summit, I was awed by the profound silence which reigned over the vast pile that crowned Mount Moriah. The sun was not yet risen; but the east blushed with a roseate purple, and the morning star was melting into its depth. Night and silence still held united empire over the city and the altar of God. I was awe-silent. I stood with my hands crossed upon my bosom and my head reverently bowed, for in the absence of man and his voice I believed angels were all around in heavenly hosts, the guardian armies of this wondrous city of David. Lances of light now shot upward and across the purple sea in the East, and fleeces of clouds, that reposed upon it like barks, catching the red rays of the yet unrisen sun, blazed like burning ships. Each moment the darkness fled, and the splendor of the dawn increased; and when I expected to see the sun appear over the battlemented heights of Mount Moriah, I was thrilled by the startling peal of the trumpets of the priests; a thousand silver trumpets blown at once from the walls of the Temple, and shaking the very foundations of the city with their mighty voice. Instantly the house-tops everywhere around were alive with worshipers. Jerusalem started, as one man, from its slumbers, and, with their faces towards the Temple, a hundred thousand men of Israel stood waiting. A second trumpet peal, clear and musical as the voice of God when he spake to our father Moses in Horeb, caused every knee to bend, and every tongue to join in the morning song of praise. The murmur of voices was like the continuous roll of the surge upon the beach, and the walls of the lofty Temple echoed it back. Simultaneously with the billow-like swell of the adoring hymn, I beheld a pillar of black smoke ascend from the midst of the Temple, and spread itself above the court like a canopy. It was accompanied by a blue wreath of lighter and more misty appearance, which threaded in and out and entwined about the other, like a silvery strand woven into a sable cord. This latter was the smoke of the incense which accompanied the burnt sacrifice. As I saw it rise higher and higher, and finally overtop the heavy cloud, which was instantly enlarged by volumes of dense smoke that rolled upward from the consuming victim, and slowly disappeared, melting into heaven, I also kneeled, remembering that on the wings of the incense went up the prayers of the people; and ere it dissolved wholly, I entrusted to it, dear father, prayers for thee and me.

The evening sacrifice is, if possible, more imposing than that of the morning. Just as the sun dips beyond the hill of Gibeah, there is heard a prolonged note of a trumpet blown from one of the western watch-towers of Zion. Its mellow tones reach farthest ear within the gates of the city. All labor at once ceases. Every man raises his face towards the summit of the house of God. A deep pause, as if all held their breath in expectation, succeeds. Suddenly the very skies seem to be riven and shaken with the thunder of the company of trumpeters that rolls wave on wave of sound, from the battlements of the Temple. The dark cloud of sacrifice ascends in solemn grandeur, and, sometimes heavier than the evening air, falls like a descending curtain around the Mount, till the whole is veiled from sight; but above it is seen to soar the purer incense to the invisible Jehovah, followed by a myriad eyes, and the utterance of a nation's prayers. As the daylight faded, the light of the altar, hidden from us by the lofty walls of the outer court of the Temple, blazed high and beacon-like, and lent a wild solemnity to the towers and pinnacles that crowned Moriah.

PANORAMA OF JERUSALEM

There was, however, my dear father, last evening, one thing which painfully marred the holy character of the sacred hour. After the blast of the silver trumpets of the Levites had ceased, and while all hearts and eyes were ascending to Jehovah with the mounting wreaths of incense, there came from the Roman castle adjoining the city of David, a loud martial clangor of brazen bugles, and other barbarian war instruments of music, while a smoke, like the smoke of sacrifice, rose from the heights of David's fortified hill. I was told that it was the Romans engaged in worshiping Jupiter. Alas! How truly now are the prophecies fulfilled, which are to be found in the Lamentations: "The Lord hath cast off his altar, he hath given up into the hands of the enemy the walls of her palaces: they have made a noise in the house of the Lord, as in the day of a solemn feast." For these things I weep, my dear father.

Nearly three hundred years have passed since we have had a prophet—that divine and youthful Malachi. Since his day, Rabbi Amos confesses that Jehovah has made no sign of having heard the prayers or heeded the sacrifices that have been offered to him in his time. I inquired of the intelligent Rabbi if it would always be thus. He replied that when Shiloh came, there would be a restoration of all things—that the glory of Jerusalem then would fill the whole earth with the splendor of the sun, and that all nations should come up from the ends of the world to worship in the Temple.

My conversation with Rabbi Amos, dear father, led me to examine the Book of the Prophet Malachi. I find that after plainly alluding to our present shame, and reproaching the priests "for causing the people to stumble," he thus prophesies: "Behold, I will send my messenger, and he shall prepare the way before me; and the Lord whom ye seek shall suddenly come to his Temple, and he shall sit as a refiner and purifier of silver, and he shall purify the sons of Levi, and purge them as gold and silver, that they may offer unto the Lord an offering in righteousness. Behold," adds the divine seer, "I will send you Elijah the prophet before the coming of the great and dreadful day of the Lord."

These words I read to-day to Rabbi Amos—indeed I was reading them when Rabbi Ben Israel came in to say that he departs to-morrow. The excellent Amos looked grave. I feared I had offended him by my boldness, and, approaching him, was about to embrace him, when I saw tears were sparkling in his eyes. He took my hand, and smiling, while a glittering drop danced down his snow-white beard and broke into liquid diamonds upon my hand, he said, "You have done no wrong, child; sit down by me and be at peace with thyself. It is too true, in this day, what the Prophet Malachi writeth, O Ben Israel," he said sadly to the Alexandrian Rabbi. "The priests of the Temple have indeed become corrupt, save a few here and there. It must have been at this day the prophet aimed his words. Save in the outward form, I fear the great body of our Levites have little more true religion and just knowledge of the one God Jehovah, than the priests of the Roman idolatry. Alas, I fear me, God regards our sacrifices with no more favor than he looks upon theirs. To-day, while I was in the Temple, and was serving at the altar with the priests, these words of Isaiah came into my thoughts and would not be put aside: 'To what purpose is the multitude of your sacrifices unto me? saith the Lord. I am full of the burnt offerings of rams, and the fat of fed beasts; and I delight not in the blood of bullocks, or of lambs, or of he-goats. Bring no more vain oblations; incense is an abomination unto me; I am weary to bear them; yea, when ye spread forth your hands I will hide mine eyes from you; yea, when ye make many prayers I will not hear; your hands are full of blood. Wash you; make you clean. Cease to do evil; learn to do well.'"

"I have noticed," said Ben Israel, "that there is less reverence now in the Temple than when I was in Jerusalem a young man; but I find that the magnificence of the ceremonies is increased."

"Yes," responded Rabbi Amos, with a look of sorrow, "yes, as the soul of piety dies out from within, they gild the outside. The increased richness of the worship is copied from the Romans. So low are we fallen! Our worship, with all its gorgeousness, is as a sepulchre white-washed to conceal the rottenness within!"

You may be convinced, my dear father, that this confession, from such a source, deeply humbled me. If, then, we are not worshiping God, what do we worship? Naught! We are worse off than our barbarian conquerors, for we have no God; while they at least have gods many and lords many, such as they are.

Since writing the last line I have been interrupted by Mary, who has brought to see me a youth, nephew of a noble Jewish ruler, who was slain by the Romans for his patriotic devotion to his country. He dwells near the Gaza gate, with his widowed mother, who is a noble lady, honored by all. Between this young man, whose name is John, and Mary, there exists a beautiful attachment, which is each day ripening into the deepest emotion. He has just returned from the vicinity of Jericho, where he has been for some days past, drawn thither by curiosity to see and hear the new prophet, who is drawing thousands into the wilderness, to listen to the eloquence that flows from his mouth. The young man had been giving Mary so interesting an account of him that she desired me also to be a listener. In my next I will write you all I heard.

Your affectionate and devoted daughter,

Adina.

LETTER III.

My Dear Father:

This morning, as I was coming from the Temple, I noticed a vast pile of edifices crowning the opposite rock, which I was told was the Tower of Antonia. It seemed to frown sternly upon the Temple; and upon its battlements glittered, at intervals, numerous Roman eagles. I had so often heard you relate historical events connected with this celebrated castle, that I regarded it with peculiar interest. You seemed to stand by my side as I gazed upon it. The insolence and power of the Roman garrison have made the beautiful walk about the base of the tower almost deserted; but of this I was not aware; and, attended only by my Ethiopian slave, Onia, I lingered to admire the splendor of the cloister once surrounding the treasure-house of the Temple, with its terraces supported by white marble pillars, fifteen cubits high, when two Roman soldiers approached. It was then that I saw I was alone. I drew my veil closely, and would have passed them rapidly, when one of them placed himself in my path, and catching hold of my veil, tried to detain me. I left it in his grasp and was flying, when the other soldier arrested me. This was in full view of the castle, and at my shrieks the barbarians in the castle laughed aloud. At this crisis appeared a young centurion, who was on horseback, coming down the rocky path that ascends the Rock of Zion, and shouting to them, he galloped forward, and with his sword put the men to immediate flight and rescued me. In order to escort me safely to the streets below, he alighted from his horse, and leading him by the rein, walked by my side. I confess to you, dear father, I had not reached the house of my relative before my prejudices against the Romans were greatly modified. I had found in one of them as courteous a person as I had ever met with among my own countrymen, and for his sake I was willing to think better of his barbaric land and people.

TOWER OF ANTONIA

While I was writing the above, a commotion without drew me to the lattice, which overlooks the street that goes out of the gate to Bethany, one of the most frequented thoroughfares in the city. The sight that met my eyes was truly imposing, but made my heart sink with shame. It was a pageant, with banners, eagles, trumpets and gilded chariots, but not the pageant of a king of Israel, like those which dazzled the streets of Jerusalem in the days of Solomon and King David; not the triumphant passage of an Israelitish prince, but of the Roman governor. Preceded by a cohort of horse, he rode in a gilded war-chariot, lolling at his ease beneath a silken shade of blue silk, fringed with gold. The horses were snowy-white, and covered with silver mail, and adorned with plumes. He was followed by another body of cavalry, and at the head of them, looking more like a ruler and prince than did the indolent Pilate, I beheld the generous centurion who had aided my escape from the two soldiers. His eye sought the lattice at which I stood, and I drew back, but not before he had seen me and saluted me. Certainly, father, this youth is noble and courteous enough to be a Jew, and should any providence cause us to meet again, I shall try to convert him from his idolatry to serve the living Jehovah.

You will remember, dear father, that I alluded to an excitement that is increasing every day, in reference to a new prophet, who is preaching in the wilderness of Jericho. For three weeks past several parties of citizens have been to the valley of Jordan to see and hear him, and have so far been carried away by him as to have been baptized of him in Jordan, confessing their sins. Among them is John, the cousin and betrothed of Mary. Upon his return we saw that his countenance was animated beyond its wont, for he is usually of a sad and gentle aspect, and that his fine eyes beamed with an ardent hope, that seemed new-born to his soul. He thus recounted to us his visit to the prophet of Jordan:

"After leaving the gate of the city I soon reached the pretty town of Bethpage, where, at the inn, I beheld several horsemen just mounting, to go in the direction of Jericho. On joining the cavalcade, I learned they were for the most part drawn out of Jerusalem on the same errand with myself. One of them, a wealthy young noble of Arimathea, was actuated by the same holy desire that burned in my bosom, a desire that we might, in the prophet who was called John, discover a man sent from God. The others were bent on commerce, on pleasure, or mere idle curiosity. As Joseph of Arimathea and I rode together, we conversed about the man we expected to see. My companion seemed to believe that he was a true prophet, for being very well read in the Scriptures, he said that the seventy weeks of Daniel were now about completed, when the Messiah was to come! I then asked him if he believed that the Messiah, who was to be a 'Prince and king and have dominion from the sea to the ends of the earth,' would come in the wilderness, clad in the skin of wild beasts? To this he replied that he could not regard this prophet as the Messiah, for when the Christ should come, he was 'suddenly to come to the Temple,' and that we should doubtless first see him there; but that he was greatly in hopes that the prophet we were going to see would prove to be the forerunner, foretold by Malachi.

"'Those who heard him,' said Joseph, as we rode into the village of Bethany, 'say that he publicly proclaims himself the forerunner of the

Messiah. The opinion of the more ignorant who have listened to him, is that it is Elijah himself, returned to the earth. Others assert that it is Enoch come down from heaven, and not a few believe him to be Isaiah.'"

At this point of the narrative of the cousin of Mary, dear father, I will close this letter. In my next I will resume his narrative, for when I have given it to you wholly, I have many things to ask you to which it gives rise in my mind. May the blessing of the God of Israel be upon thee, my dearest father!

Adina.

LETTER IV.

My Dear Father:

I have had the pleasure to-day, not only of hearing from you, but of being assured of your continued welfare. The messages of parental affection contained in your letter are cherished in my heart.

You need not fear, my dear father, that I shall be carried away from the faith of Israel by any strange doctrines. I will take counsel by your wisdom, and be cautious how I venture in my inquiries upon sacred ground.

In my last letter I commenced giving you the narrative of John, with which I shall now proceed.

"Having passed out of the city of Jericho, my friend of Arimathea and myself crossed the plain toward Jordan. The morning was balmy; the sun made all nature glad. The dew reflected a myriad lesser suns, and the earth appeared strewn with diamonds. For a little way the road lay between fields of corn and gardens, but soon it crossed the open plain, on which were droves of wild asses, which lifted their small, spirited heads on our approach, eyed us with timid curiosity, and then bounded off to the wilderness southward with the speed of antelopes. As the great body of the people took their way obliquely across the plain, we knew the prophet must be in that direction. We at length found him on the banks of Jordan, below the landing and ford, which is opposite Jericho, on the great caravan road to Balbec.

"We drew near a dark mass of human beings which we had beheld afar off, assembled around a small eminence near the river. Upon it, raised a few cubits taller than their heads, stood a man upon whom all eyes were fixed, and to whose words every ear was attentive. His clear, rich, earnest tones had reached us as we approached, before we could distinguish what he said. He was a young man not above thirty, with a countenance such as the medallions of Egypt give to Joseph of our nation, once their prince. His hair was long, and wildly free about his neck; he wore a loose sack of camel's hair, and his right arm was naked to the shoulder. His attitude was as free and commanding as that of a Caucasian warrior, yet every gesture was gentle and graceful. With all his ringing and persuasive eloquence there was an air of the deepest humility upon his countenance, combined with an expression of the holiest enthusiasm. His theme was the Messiah.

"'Oh, Israel, return unto the Lord thy God, for thou hast fallen by thine iniquity,' he was saying as we came up, as if in continuation of what had gone before. 'Take with you words, and turn unto the Lord, and say unto him: Take away all iniquity, and receive us graciously. Behold, he cometh who will heal your backsliding, and will love you freely. And it shall come to pass that whosoever shall call on the name of the Lord shall be delivered, for beside him there is no Savior.'

"'Of whom speaketh the prophet these things?' asked one who stood near me.

"'Of Messiah—listen!' answered him a Scribe near, as if not pleased to have his attention interrupted by this side talk. 'His words are plain. Hear him.'

"'Blow ye the trumpet in Zion, for the day of the Lord cometh,' continued the prophet, in a voice like that of a silver trumpet; 'for, behold, the day is at hand when I will bring again the captivity of Judah. Put ye in the sickle, for the harvest is ripe. The day is at hand when the Lord shall roar out of Zion and utter his voice from Jerusalem.'

"'Art thou not Elias?' asked one aloud.

"'I am he of whom it is written. The voice of one crying in the wilderness, make straight a highway for our God. The day of the Lord is at hand. I am but the herald who is sent before to prepare the way of the Lord.'

"'Art thou not the Messiah?' asked a woman who stood near him, and seemed to worship his very lips.

"'He who cometh after me is mightier than I, whose shoes I am not worthy to bear,' he responded, in an exultant tone, strangely at variance with his words. 'Therefore, repent ye, repent ye, take words and return unto the Lord our God. Repent and be baptized for the remission of your sins.' Then he added, turning to some of the priests, 'Behold, even now is the axe laid unto the root of the trees; every tree, therefore, that bringeth not forth good fruit is hewn down and cast into the fire.'

"'Master,' said a Levite, 'dost thou speak these things to us, who are of Israel, or to these Gentiles and Samaritans?' for there were not a few Roman soldiers among the multitude, drawn hither by curiosity, and also many people from Samaria.

"'Go and cry in the ears of Jerusalem, saith the Lord, for my people have committed two evils; they have forsaken me, the fountain of living waters, and hewn them out cisterns, broken cisterns, that can hold no water. And yet thou sayest, O Israel, thou hast not sinned. Thine own wickedness shall correct thee, and thy backsliding shall reprove thee. Repent and do works meet for repentance, every one of you, for ye have polluted the land; neither say, Where is the Lord that brought us up out of the land of Egypt? Trust not to lying words, saying, The Temple of the Lord, the Temple of the Lord, the Temple of the Lord! Ye have made it a den of robbers. Your sacrifices therein are become an abomination.'

"'This would touch us who are priests, master,' said a priest, with a crimson brow. 'We are not robbers.'

"'Thus saith the Lord,' answered the youthful prophet, as if it were God himself speaking from Horeb, so that we trembled: 'Woe be unto the pastors that destroy my sheep. How is the gold become dim! how is the most fine gold changed! The precious sons of Zion, comparable to fine gold, how are they esteemed? Woe unto you, ye priests, for ye have transgressed. My people have transgressed for lack of knowledge. Therefore doth the land mourn, and every one that dwelleth therein languisheth. Therefore do swearing and lying, and killing and stealing, and committing adultery, break out in the land, because there is no truth, nor mercy, nor knowledge of God in the land. Woe unto you, ye priests!'

"Many of the Levites then turned and left him and went away greatly murmuring; and they would gladly have done the prophet a mischief, but they feared the multitude, who said he had spoken only the truth of them.

"'But the elders of Israel, who are not priests, who spring from Abraham, shall be saved by Abraham, master?' asserted, or rather inquired, a rich ruler of our city, after the tumult caused by the withdrawal of the Levites had a little subsided. The youthful prophet rested his dark eyes, like two suns, upon the old man's face, and said impressively, 'Begin not to say within yourself, We have Abraham to our father; for I say unto you,' he added, pointing to the pebbles at his feet, 'that God is able of these stones to raise up children unto Abraham. He is of Abraham who doth righteousness; therefore repent, and bring forth fruits meet for repentance.'

"Here was heard some murmuring among a group of many Pharisees and Sadducees at these words, when, sending his lightning glance towards them, as if he could read their very hearts, he cried:

"'O generation of vipers! Who hath warned you to flee from the wrath to come? The day cometh when he who is to come shall sit as a purifier by his furnace. Bring forth, therefore, fruits meet for repentance. Turn thy heart from wickedness, that thou mayest be saved. Repent ye, for the kingdom of heaven is at hand.

"'Hear, O Israel! Am I a God at hand and not a God afar off? saith the Lord. Hear ye the message of the Most High, for the day hath come when Jehovah shall once more visit the earth and talk face to face with his creatures. Behold, the day hath come, saith the Lord, that I will raise unto David a righteous branch, and a king to reign and prosper, who shall execute judgment and justice on the earth.

"'Behold, the day hath come, saith the Lord, in which Judah shall be saved, and Israel shall dwell safely; when I will set up shepherds over them, which shall feed them, and they shall lack nothing.

"'Arise, shine, for thy light is come, and the glory of the Lord is risen upon thee! Darkness covereth the earth, and gross darkness the people, as saith Esaias; but the Lord shall rise upon thee, and his glory shall be seen upon thee. The Gentiles shall come to his light, and kings to the brightness of his rising. He shall be called the Lord of our righteousness, and shall be a crown of glory in the hand of the Lord, and a royal diadem in the hand of thy God. The Spirit of the Lord is upon me to proclaim the acceptable year of his coming. He hath set me a watchman upon thy walls, O Israel, and I may neither hold my peace day nor night, nor keep silence, nor seek rest, till he come, who hath sent me forth his messenger before his face. How can I refrain from my message of joy? How shall I not speak of his fame? Incline your ear and come unto him. Hear, and your soul shall live.

"'Sing unto the Lord a new song, and his praise from the ends of the earth; for thus saith God the Lord, I have put my spirit upon him; a bruised reed shall he not break, and the smoking flax shall he not quench. I, the Lord, saith Jehovah, addressing the Only Begotten, I have called thee in righteousness, and will hold thy hand and keep thee, and will give thee for a covenant of the people, for a light of the Gentiles, to open the blind eyes, to bring out the prisoners from the prison. I have made him, my first-born, higher than the kings of the earth. Look unto him, and be ye saved, all the ends of the earth. The Lord of Hosts is his name, the Holy One of Israel.'

"All this was spoken with an enthusiasm and fire that made every pulse bound.

"Such," said John, "was the extraordinary style of this mighty prophet's preaching. I fancied I had only to look around to behold the Messiah. The immense multitude stood awed and silent when he had ceased. Leaving the eminence, he said, and I thought he fixed his eyes upon me, 'Ye who desire to be baptized for the remission of sins, that your hearts may be cleansed for the visitation of this Holy One of God, follow me to the river side.' Thousands obeyed, and I one of the first. I trembled all over with a sweet pleasure, when he took me by the hand, and asked me if I believed in him who was to come, and would prepare the way for his abode in my heart by being baptized, which rite also was to be a sign and pledge that when I should behold the Shiloh rising, I should acknowledge him. Not less than one thousand were baptized by him that day in Jordan, confessing their sins, and hopes of pardon through the name of the Unknown One, who was soon to come.

"After the baptism, the whole company dispersed in groups, and the prophet returned into the wilderness till the cool of the evening, where his repast was locusts and the wild honey of the desert."

With this, dear father, I close my long letter. I make no comments. I will only say that my expectations are actively awake, and that I am looking, with thousands of others, for the near advent of the Messiah.

Your daughter,

Adina.

———————————————————————

LETTER V.

My Dear Father:

"After the prophet had ended his second discourse, and baptized full two hundred more in the sparkling waters of Jordan," resumed the eloquent cousin of Mary, "he sent them away to the city to lodge and buy meat; for few, in their eagerness to hear him, had brought provisions with them. Many, before leaving him, drew near to receive his blessing of love, and it was touching to see venerable men, with locks shining like silver, and leaning upon the staff, bend their aged heads before the youthful Elias, as if in acknowledgment of his divine commission. Mothers also brought their infants, that he might bless them; and youths and maidens knelt reverently at his feet in tears of love and penitence. Calmly he stood upon the green shores, like an angel alighted upon earth, and blessed them in words all new to our ears, but which thrilled to our hearts with some secret power that agitated us with trembling joy.

"'In the name of the Lamb of God I bless thee!'

"'What can be the meaning of these words?' asked Mary, with her gentle earnestness. Her betrothed could only reply that he knew not.

"At length, one after another, the multitude departed, save a few who encamped beneath trees on the banks of the river. Joseph of Arimathea and I were left almost alone standing near the prophet, and regarding him with reverential curiosity. The sun was just disappearing over the distant towers of Jericho, and painting with the richest purple the hills between the river and Jerusalem. Jordan, catching its reddening radiance, rolled past like a river of liquid gold embanked in emerald. The brow of the prophet, lighted up by a sun-ray that shone between the branches of a pomegranate tree, seemed like the face of Moses when he came down from Sinai, a glory of light. He appeared rapt in heavenly meditation, and we stood silent and gazed upon him, not daring to speak. At length he turned towards us, smiled, and, saluting us, grasped the crook or staff on which he had been leaning—for he was weary and pale with his labors of the day—and slowly walked down the shore in the direction of the wilderness. He had not advanced many steps when I felt an irresistible impulse to follow him. I therefore said to my companion:

"'Let us follow him, and learn more of these great things which we have this day heard.'

"We proceeded slowly after him, as he moved in a contemplative mood along the desert path. The sun had already gone down, and the full moon rose on the opposite shore, and the prophet stopped as if to gaze upon its autumnal beauty. We drew near to him. He beheld us, but did not avoid us; seeing which, I advanced with timid confidence, and said:

"'Holy prophet of the Most High God, wilt thou permit two young men of Israel to speak to thee? for our hearts yearn towards thee with love. And chiefly would we inquire of thee touching the advent of the mighty Personage whose near coming thou dost foretell?'

"'Friends,' said the prophet, in a calm and serene manner, 'I am a dweller in the desert, and alone, from choice. I approach men only to proclaim my message. The delights of earth are not for me. My mission is one. Its duration is short. Its aim worthy the greatest prophet of God, yet am I, the least of them, not worthy to be called a prophet; and before the splendor of him whom I announce to the world, I am the dust of the balance. If thou hast sought me to search after knowledge, come and sit down with me upon this rock, and let me hear what thou hast to ask of me, that I may answer thee and go my way.'

"This was said softly, gently, almost sadly, and in a tone that made me love him more and more. I could have cast myself upon his bosom and wept there. We seated ourselves, one on either side of him. The scene and the hour were well fitted for such a converse as we were about to hold. The broad disc of the moon poured a flood of orange-tinted radiance full upon us, and lent a hallowed softness to the divine countenance of the youthful prophet. The Jordan, dark as India's dye, darted swiftly past at our feet, between its deeply-shaded banks, sending up to our ears the faintest murmur of its pebbly passage. Above our heads swelled the vaulted arch of the Temple of Jehovah, with its myriad of altar fires. Behind us stretched the desert waste, cheerless and yet grand in its desolate distances.

"Afar off rose upon the air, and was borne to us at intervals, the voice of a singer in one of the camps; and near us, upon an acacia tree, sat a solitary bulbul, which ceaselessly sang its sweet and varied hymn to the listening moon.

"'All things praise God; shall we be silent?' said the prophet. 'Let us sing the evening hymn of the Temple.' He then commenced, in a rich, melodious chant, such as I have never heard from the priests, our sacred psalm to the whole creation of God. We joined our voices with his, and the tide of praise floated over the waters, and echoed and re-echoed from the opposing shores, as if the banks and stream, trees, hills and sky had found voice as well as we:

"'Praise! praise! praise ye the Lord!Praise him in the heights! Praise him in the seas!Praise him, men of Israel! Praise ye the Lord!For he exalteth high his people,And reigneth evermore!

"'Praise him, all ye angels! Praise him, all ye hosts!Praise him, sun and moon, and all ye stars of light!Praise him, fire and hail! Praise him, storm and snows!For he judgeth the earth in righteousness,And reigneth evermore!

"'Praise! praise! praise ye the Lord!Praise him, winged fowl, and herds, cattle, and all beasts!Praise him, kings and people, princes, priests and judges!Praise him, youths and maidens, old men and children!

"'Praise the name, let them praise the name,Praise the name of the Lord God of Hosts!For his name alone is excellent,His glory above the heavens;Israel is his first-born—a people well-beloved!Praise! let Israel, therefore, praise him!Praise him evermore,Evermore,Ever, evermore!'

"Never shall I forget the effect produced upon my inmost being by this hymn. The prophet sang as if he were leading a choir of angels. My heart leaped at the chorus, as if it would break out, take wing and leave the earth. When we called on the winds and the fowls of the air to praise Jehovah with us, the thrilling voice of the bulbul seemed to pour from its throat a wilder, richer, more joyous tide of song, and the audible wind bent the adoring trees, and mingled its mystic whispers with the psalm of men. Surely, thought I, it is good for me to be here, for this is none other than the gate of Paradise!

"After a few moments' silence, the prophet spoke and said:

"'You sought me, brethren of Israel; can I do aught for you?'

"'We would hear more, great prophet, touching this mighty One who is to come after thee,' said Joseph.

"'I can tell thee but little, my brethren, save what thou hast heard from me this day. The future is veiled. I bear a message, indeed, but I may not break the seal and read. To you it will be given to know what is now unknown to me. If it be permitted me to see him, it will be but for a brief space, for when he cometh I depart—my errand is done. Blessed are those who live to witness his glory, and to hear the gracious voice of God that proceeds from his anointed lips.'

"'And when will be his advent, and with what form and power cometh this divine Being?' I asked.

"'As a man, but not with comeliness of form that men should desire him. His appearance will be humble, lowly and meek.'

"'Yet you said to-day, Rabbi,' I continued, 'that his power should be infinite, and that of his kingdom there should be no end. You spoke of the glory of his dominions, and the humiliation of Gentile kings beneath his sceptre.'

"'This I cannot explain—it is a mystery to me. I speak as God, by whom I am sent, gives me utterance. I know that he who cometh after me is greater than I, the latchet of whose shoes I am not worthy to unloose.'

"'You taught us this evening, holy prophet, that he would be the Lord from heaven; and yet that Esaias saith he will be despised and rejected of men, wounded for our transgressions, and bruised for our iniquities.'

"'The spirit of God teaches me that these words apply to Shiloh; but I cannot comprehend how these things can be,' he answered, with deep sadness.

"'May I remind you, good Rabbi,' said Joseph, 'that you taught us how this Divine Personage should die, though Lord of life, and be numbered in his death with transgressors, though the Holy One of God?'

"'And such will be the events that are to happen; but seek not to know what no man hath had revealed to him. The divine Messiah himself must be his own interpreter. Blessed will be the eyes that behold him, and listen to the wisdom of his mouth, and keep the law of his lips.'

"'May I ask you, holy prophet of the Lord,' said Joseph, 'how is it that he whom you are sent by God to bear witness to can be the Deliverer of Israel, when you predict for him so sad a fate? Messiah is to restore Jerusalem and the glory of the Temple, so saith Esaias, so say Ezra and Jeremiah. We therefore, in the Messiahs of the prophets, have looked for a powerful potentate, who shall reign in Jerusalem over the whole earth and subdue all nations.'

"'His kingdom is not of this earth,' answered the prophet, impressively.

"'How then can we interpret the prophet David, who maketh the Lord to say: "I have set my King upon my holy hill of Zion"? Also, how shall we interpret those sayings of Esaias who, prophesying of the blessed Christ of God, hath these words: "Of the increase of his government and peace there shall be no end, upon the throne of David, and upon his kingdom, to order it and to establish it with judgment and with justice, from henceforth, even forever"?'

"'I know not. These secrets are with God. This I know, that the least child and the lowliest hireling that liveth in the day of Messias is greater than I. I am the last of the prophets. It is for me to open the last door that leads out from the night of prophecy into the glorious dawn of the day of fulfillment; but I am not permitted to enter beyond the threshold, or share in its blessings. All who come after me will be preferred before me. But let me rejoice that the day-star is about to rise, though his beams shine on all the earth but me!' This was said with the most touching pathos.

"We were both deeply moved, I myself even to tears. I sank on my knees, and kissing his hand, bathed it with my tears.

"He gently raised me, and said in a sweet voice:

"'Brother beloved, thou shalt see him to whom I bear witness, and he will love thee, and thou shalt repose in his bosom!' I burst into tears, and, rising, I walked a little ways apart, and lifting up my eyes toward heaven, I prayed the God of our fathers that I might be found worthy of this blessed honor.

"'And shall I also behold this mighty Son of God?' asked Joseph, with solicitude.

"The prophet took his hand in his, and fixing upon him his eyes of prophetic brightness, said slowly, and in tones awe-inspiring and painfully sorrowful:

"'Thou shalt one day bear him in thine arms, and lay him upon a couch which thou hast prepared for thine own repose. Thou knowest not now what I say, but thou shalt remember it when it cometh to pass!'

"When he had thus spoken, he arose, and waving his hand to us both, he walked rapidly away towards the darkening desert.

"'Didst thou hear him?' at length, after some minutes' pause, asked Joseph of me. 'What can his words mean? They are prophetic of some fearful event. His eyes betrayed some terrible meaning. My heart is troubled.'

"'And mine rejoiceth.' I answered. 'We shall see him! I shall be near him! Oh, if he be like this sweet prophet of God, I shall love him with all my soul's being! How wonderful that we are to be thus associated with this Divine Person! Welcome the hour of his blessed advent!'

"'Wilt thou welcome the advent of a sufferer?' said a voice so near that it startled us by its abruptness, and, looking round, we saw, standing within the shadow of a wild olive tree, a young man who was a stranger, but to whom I afterwards became deeply attached. His face was pale and intellectual, and his form slight but of the most symmetrical elegance. His question at once made me sorrowful, for it recalled the sad prophecy of Esaias.

"'He is also to be king and monarch of the world, and infinitely holy and good,' I said. 'If thou hast been near, thou hast heard the glorious things the prophet has spoken of him.'

"'I have been near—I was reclining beneath this tree when you seated yourselves there. Be not deceived; the divine Man who is to come is to be a man of sorrows and acquainted with grief. He is to be rejected by Israel and despised by Judah. Those whom he comes to bless will despise him for his lowliness and obscurity. His life will be a life of tears, and toil, and heaviness of heart, and he will at last be cut off from among the living, with the ignominy due only to a transgressor. Dost thou welcome the advent of a sufferer?'

"'But how knowest thou this? Art thou a prophet?' I asked with surprise and admiration.

"'No, brother, but I have read the prophets. I heard, moreover, the words of this holy man sent from God, and he dwells more on the humility of the Christ than on his kingly grandeur. Believe me, the kingdom of Shiloh is not of this world. It cannot be of this world, if such is to be his life and death; and that it is to be his life, Esaias clearly states. Let me read to you his words.' He then took a roll of parchment from his bosom, and read by the clear tropical moonlight, that mysterious and inexplicable passage which beginneth with the words: 'Who hath believed our report?' When he had ended, he resumed: 'This is not the history of a prosperous earthly monarch, but rather the painful record of a life of humiliation, of shame, and of contempt.'

"'But thou dost not say, brother,' said Joseph, with some warmth, 'that the sacred Person borne witness to by this prophet is to be an object of contempt?'

"'Does not Esaias say that he will be despised, beaten with stripes, rejected of men, imprisoned, and put to death like a transgressor of the law?'

"'There can be no question but that Esaias speaks of the Messiah,' I remarked.

"'This prophet of Jordan now bears full testimony to Esaias, and plainly maketh application of his words to him whom he has come beforehand to proclaim,' answered the young man, with singularly graceful eloquence in all he said. 'Let us who have been baptized this day for the remission of our sins, expect a Messiah of sorrows, not a conquering prince. Let us behold one who is to humble himself beneath the yoke of human infirmities, that he may be exalted, and draw all men after him to a kingdom in the heavens.'

"'But the throne of David—' objected Joseph.

"'Is at the right hand of God.'

"'But Jerusalem, and its rule over the nations—'

"'Jerusalem that is above, will be over all.'

"'But his kingdom that is to be everlasting—'

"'Is where life is everlasting. How can he rule an everlasting realm here on earth without living forever, and his subjects also? Read not the prophets so? As Adam fell and lost paradise, so Messias, like a second Adam, must, as man, humble himself, in human nature, to repurchase the kingdom of paradise for the race of man. It is this kingdom which this prophet proclaims as being at hand. He being the bearer of our iniquities, we shall thereby escape their chastisement. Healed by his stripes, we shall be free from our sins. Laid upon him will be the transgressions of the world; and by one mighty sacrifice of himself, thus laden, as a sin-offering, he shall offer an atonement to make one with Jehovah the great family of Adam. Such is to be our looked-for Messiah. Alas, while we look for him, let us mingle tears with our gladness, that one so holy and excellent should be destined to endure these things for our sakes; and when we behold him, let us sink at his feet in grateful adoration of his love.'

"When the young man had spoken, he walked away. Impelled by an unconquerable impulse, I followed, and took him in my arms, and embracing him, said: 'Of a truth thou art a prophet! Thy words come home to my heart like the echo of ancient prophecy.'

"'Nay. I have learned these things from the study of the Scripture,' he said, with angelic candor and modesty. 'But I have been aided, how much I have no words to tell thee, by one who hath wisdom and truth abiding in him above all men, and whom it is my happiness to have my bosom friend, as he is near my own age. If I am wise, or virtuous, or good, or know the Scriptures, it is that he hath been my counselor and teacher.'

"'What is his name?' I asked, 'for I also would go and learn of him.'

"'He withdraws from the public eye, and hath little converse but with few, and shuns all notice. Without his permission I could not take thee to him.'

"'What is his appearance, and where doth he dwell?' I inquired, more deeply interested.

"'He abides at present at Bethany, my own city. He is so beloved by us, that we detain him as our guest. But he dwelleth at other times with his mother, a holy widow of great sanctity and matronly dignity, living at Nazareth in humble condition, and he contributes by labor to her support, with the most exemplary filial piety. No person ever approaches and speaks with him without leaving a wiser and better man.'

"'Verily,' said Joseph and I together, 'you have only increased our desire to behold him. His appearance must be noble.'

"'There sits upon his brow a serene dignity, tempered with mildness, that commands the respect of age, and wins the confiding love of childhood. His eyes beam with a light, calm and pure, as if shining from interior holy thoughts, and they rest upon you, when he speaks, with a tenderness that is like the dewy light of the young mother's gaze, when she bends in silent happiness and tears over the face of her first-born. His face is one soft sunshine of smiling rays, tempered in an indescribable manner with a settled look of sadness, an almost imperceptible shade of permanent sorrow, that seems to foreshadow a life of trial and suffering.'

"'He must be another prophet,' said Joseph, with deep earnestness.

"'He does not prophesy, nor preach,' answered the young man.

"'What is his name?' I asked.

"'Jesus, the Nazarene.'

"As the young man was then about to move away, I asked him his name, as he had greatly drawn out my heart towards him, and I felt that if I could be his friend, and the friend of the wise young man of Nazareth, I should be perfectly happy and have no other desire—save, indeed, to live till the Messiah came, that I might behold him, and lay my head upon his sacred bosom.

"'My name is Lazarus, the Scribe,' he answered."

"What?" interrupted Mary. "Then I know him well. He is the brother of Mary and Martha, my friends at Bethany, where I passed a week last year, just before the Passover."

"The next day," continued John, "we renewed our acquaintance, and after three days departed together homeward. Upon arriving at Bethany, Lazarus learned that his friend had gone to Cana, in Galilee, on a visit with his mother, to the house of one of her kinfolk, whose daughter is soon to be married."

Having now, my dear father, communicated to you all that John related to us, you will see what grounds there are to look upon the prophet of Jordan as a man sent from God, or to believe that he is the true Elias, whom Malachi hath foretold, and who, as the most learned of the Scribes say, must first come to proclaim the approach of the Prince of Peace, the Shiloh of Israel's hopes.

The account brought by John has set Rabbi Amos to studying the Prophets, and indeed all men are looking into them with interest unknown before. May God be indeed about to bless his people, and remember his inheritance!

Your affectionate daughter,

Adina.

LETTER VI.

My Dear Father:

Your letter, dear father, commands me to banish this "novelty" from my mind, and continue humbly to worship Jehovah after the manner of our fathers. I trust this I shall ever do, my dear father; and did I discover in this prophet any disposition to bring in a new faith, opposed to the ancient faith of Abraham, I should tremble to entertain it for a moment. You say that this man must be "a false and base prophet," or he would not herald a master so low and despised as he professes will be the Christ he bears witness to. "The kingdom of Messias is not a kingdom of repentance and humiliation," you add, "but one of victory, of glory and dominion."

This cut is designed after the model prepared by the student and traveler, Sir James Ferguson.

How can I write to you, my dear father, that which is now rushing to my pen, after such an expression of your sentiments as you have made in this extract from your letter? But I know you are wise, and will not evade truth, in whatever form it may offer itself to you, and I, therefore, with confidence in your justice and wisdom, will faithfully make known to you the events relating to the prophet which have transpired.

You will remember how that John, Mary's cousin, stated that many priests and others were offended at the plain preaching of the prophet whom they went out into the wilderness to see. When they returned to Jerusalem, and made known to the other members of the House of the Priests what had been spoken against them, by the application to them of the words of Esaias and Jeremias, and other prophets, there arose at once a great outcry against him. At length Annas, who is High Priest with Caiaphas, sent two of the most learned men of the Temple, Levites of weight of character, to invite the prophet to Jerusalem; for Annas is a wise man, and not easily carried away by popular feeling; and, as Rabbi Amos hath told me, he is disposed to look upon the preaching of this John with a serious and reverential eye. The messengers returned after the fifth day, and made their report openly in the Court of the Temple, where the High Priests sat to receive them. At length, the assembly being convened, the two learned and venerable Levites both rose up, and declared that they had delivered the message to John, the son of Zacharias, the prophet of Jordan, and that his answer was given with the reverence due to the station of the High Priest who had sent to him.

"'Go and say to the noble High Priest,' said he, 'that I am the voice of one crying in the wilderness, as it is written in the book of the words of Esaias the prophet, who, foreseeing my day, saith, "The voice of one crying in the wilderness, Prepare ye the way of the Lord, make his paths straight." He who would hear my testimony to him who is to come after me, let him seek me in the wilderness, whence only I am commanded to lift up my voice till Shiloh come.'"

When the priests heard this answer they were greatly enraged, and many fiercely cried one thing and many another; some that he should be sought out and stoned to death for defying the High Priest; others, that he should be accused to the Procurator, Pontius Pilate, Governor of Judea, as a seditious and dangerous person, and fermenter of insurrections. Caiaphas was of the latter opinion. But the milder Annas viewed the whole matter in a different light, and said:

"Men and brethren, let nothing be done hastily. If this man be a false prophet, he will soon perish, and we shall hear no more of him. If, peradventure, as it would appear, he is sent from God, let us not make haste to do him a mischief, lest, haply, we be found contending against the Lord of Hosts."

This moderation found favor with but few, and of these few, Rabbi Amos was one. But if the priests who thronged the outer court, in presence of the High Priest, were deeply moved at the report of the prophet's answer, their excitement became well-nigh uncontrollable when both Melchi and Heli, their messengers, rose up, waving their hands for silence, and declared that, after having listened to the prophet to whom they had been sent, they were convinced of the truth of his words, and of his divine commission, and had been baptized of him in Jordan, confessing their sins!

Only the sanctity of the Temple prevented the five hundred priests rushing upon them and smiting them when they heard this. They were at once placed under arrest by order of the High Priest, Caiaphas, for acting in a manner unbecoming a priest of the Most High God. The people who had heard John preach, however, were only prevented from rescuing the two priests by the presence of a guard of Roman soldiers, for which Caiaphas promptly sent.

From this account, my dear father, you can form some idea of the excitement which the preaching of this new prophet is producing among all classes.

If the Prince of Glory should, indeed, suddenly appear, there could be scarcely more excitement, though it would be of a different nature.

As next week Rabbi Amos does not serve in his course in the Temple, and as he will have some affairs that take him to Gilgal, he has yielded to the desire of his daughter Mary and myself to accompany him; for he does not conceal from us that he shall make it a point to visit and hear the prophet, as it will be but two hours' travel from Gilgal to the place where he preaches. You will, I fear me, object to this journey. But if the worship of our fathers has nothing to fear from falsehood, it surely has naught to fear from truth; and in either case I, as a true daughter of Israel, have nothing to fear. If the prophet teach what is false, I shall remain true; and if he teach that which is true, shall I not be the gainer?

One thing is clear—if the Christ that John prophesies be the true Son of the Highest, and is in reality to make his appearance ere long, in humiliation and poverty, his rejection by the High Priests, and by the rich and powerful of Judah, is certain. May God, then, remove blindness from our eyes, that, if this be the very Messias indeed, Israel may recognize their king when he cometh, and not do so fearful a thing in their pride as to reject him openly.

You will remember the young Roman centurion, to whose courtesy I was indebted for rescuing me from the rudeness of the two Gentile soldiers. He has preserved, since then, acquaintance with Rabbi Amos, who speaks of him with respect; and as he has of late expressed some interest in knowing what the studies are which occupy the Rabbi so constantly when he calls to see him, the Rabbi sent for me to come into the marble hall of the corridor, where they sat by the fountain under the shade of the acacia, which Amos says you took with your own hands from Isaiah's grave and planted here, many years ago, and which I, therefore, call "my father's tree."

"Come hither, Adina," said my uncle, in his benevolent tones; "here you behold a noble Roman youth whom you must be too generous to have forgotten." I bowed and scarcely lifted my eyelids from the tesselated floor, for there was a fire in the glance of the handsome youth that they could not encounter. He said some words of salutation; but I only heard the voice, which fell upon my heart with a strange vibration, like the effects of music. "The Roman centurion," continued Amos, "hath desired to know something of the sacred books of our nation, of which he saith he hath heard much; and of the prophecies, from which he believes the famed Sibylline books were composed."

Then, turning to the centurion, "Here is an Egyptian maiden, who can interpret for thee in the idiom of Grecia, or of Italia, and I will place the sacred roll in her hands while I listen. Come Adina, open and read the beginning of the Book of Moses."

To this narrative the youthful warrior listened with the profoundest respect and attention. He asked if the Messias had yet come who was to restore all things; and, if not, when he was to be looked for. This inquiry led to a conversation upon the preaching of John in the wilderness and his predictions of the near advent of Shiloh. Rabbi Amos, seeing that he was becoming deeply interested in the subject, made me turn to the particular prophecies of Daniel, Esaias, David and others, and read them to him; both those which described, in golden words, the glory and dominion of his power, and those which represented him as despised and rejected. The young man remained some time very thoughtful. At length he said, with animation: "I can now comprehend why men run into the wilderness. I should like to hear this prophet."

When Amos told him that he contemplated journeying to Gilgal the next week, and intended to visit the desert to hear him, he at once asked permission to be of his company, saying:

"I will accompany you with a squadron of horse, as the roads are not safe; for no longer ago than yesterday we received a rumor that the celebrated robber chief, Barabbas, at the head of a large band, has made his appearance again on the hills between Ephraim and Jericho."

It is therefore decided, dear father, that we leave early next week for Jericho and Gilgal. On my return I shall not fail to write you without delay. Till then withhold your judgment, and have confidence in mine. With holy aspirations for the coming of the kingdom of David and the restoration of his throne in Zion, I remain, with filial love, your daughter,

Adina.

LETTER VII.

My Dear Father:

You will recollect that in my last epistle I made mention of our intention to go to Gilgal, where John, the betrothed of Mary, was to meet us and accompany us to Jordan.

It was faint dawn when we rose from our couches to prepare for the journey. The mules upon which we were to ride were brought into the court by the two swarthy Gibeonite serfs whom Rabbi Amos holds in his service, and caparisoned with rich saddles covered with Persian saddle-cloths, embroidered with gold. The two pack mules were also made ready, on one of which was the traveling equipage of my cousin Mary and myself, which Rabbi Amos smilingly said took up more space than the goods and traveling wares of a Damascus merchant. At sunrise, after we had kneeled upon the housetop, in view of the Temple, and sent up our prayers with its sacrifices and clouds of ascending incense, we descended to the court-yard to mount for the road.

The morning was bright and cheerful, with the golden sun pouring its light over temple and tower, castle and roof, wall and rampart, hill and grove, valley and brook. As we turned the street leading to the Sheep Gate, we passed the house of Caiaphas, the High Priest, whom I saw standing upon the marble porch of his superb palace. He was not arrayed in his sumptuous robes, with the breast-plate of dazzling stones, and kingly cap, as I had seen him in the Temple, but was dressed in a flowing black robe, over which was thrown a scarf of white linen; and upon his snow-white locks he wore a scarlet hood, a dress common to all the priests, so that if I had not recognized him by his tall and commanding form and flowing white hair and piercing eye, as he surveyed us, I should have known that it was the High Priest.

A little further on we met a party coming from the country beyond Kedron, with large cages upon their mules, laden with turtle doves and young pigeons, which they were carrying to the Temple, to be sold there for sacrifices. My heart pitied the innocent things, whose blue, pretty heads were thrust by the dozen through the rough bars of their prison-houses, as they cast their soft eyes up at me, as if asking me to deliver them from their bondage. As Mary was riding behind me, in order to let the laden mules pass with their immense cages, one of the turtle doves, affrighted by the noise of the streets, extricated itself from between the bars, and spreading its wings, flew into the air, and then taking its flight for the country, soared far above the city walls and disappeared in the distance. I felt rejoiced at the innocent bird's escape, and sent my good wishes for its safe return to its lodge in the wilderness. Just before we reached the Sheep Gate, by which we were to gain the Jericho road, we met a poor blind man leading a lamb, or rather being led by a tame lamb. He also had two pigeons in his bosom. He was asked by Rabbi Amos, who knew him, whither he was going. He answered that he was going to the Temple to sacrifice them. "Nay," said Amos, with surprise, "thou wilt not sacrifice thy lamb, Bartimeus?"

"It is an offering to God, Rabbi Amos."

"But thy lamb leadeth thee everywhere. It is eyes to thee. Thou canst not do without it. And thy doves? Thou earnest by them many a mite in a day, they are so well taught in cunning and pleasant tricks to please children. If thou wilt sacrifice, spare these so needful to thee, and here is money to buy doves and another lamb," answered my benevolent uncle.

"Hear what I have to say," answered Bartimeus. "My father became sick and was likely to die. The next day my mother, who has nourished my childhood and loved me, though I was born blind, with all her heart, was also taken sick. The same night my little daughter, my little blind daughter, whose face I never saw, and who never saw her father's face, was sick nigh unto death. My father, my mother, my child, are now restored, and in my joy I am on my way to the Temple, to offer these gifts of God to him. It will not be hard to part with them, since, in giving all that I have, I but show my love to God."

With these words he went on, the lamb, obeying the string which he held, softly moving on before; while I could see the sightless eyes of the righteous son and pious father trickle tears, as he kissed and kissed again the precious doves that lay in his bosom. This little occurrence made me sad; yet I honored the resolute piety of this poor man, whose eyes, though they saw not men, seemed to see God and feel his presence. There is still humble piety in the land, my dear father, and finding it not among the proud and splendid priests, we must look for it in the hearts of the poor and humble, like Bartimeus.

Once outside the gates, the air blew fresh from the hills of olives. After being so long confined within the walls and narrow streets, it seemed to me that I had just broken out of my cage, like the pretty, blue-headed turtle dove, and I felt like winging my way, too, to the free deserts.

We had hardly reached the place where the two roads meet, when we heard to the west the sound of the galloping of a large body of horse, and the next moment the young Roman centurion came in sight, riding at the head of a troop of horse, whose martial appearance, with the ringing of their armor and the melody of their bugles, made my blood leap. Æmilius looked like a prince, and his burnished armor shone in the sun like armor of fire. At his side rode a youth who bore the eagle of his band, but the centurion himself carried in his hand only the badge of his rank, which was a vine-rod bound with rings of gold. He saluted us with that courtesy which distinguishes his every motion, and then dividing his troop into two bodies, half of whom, trotting on ahead, led the van, and the other half, falling behind, served as a rear-guard. He then gave the word to move forward.

Farewell, dear father, till my next, when I will resume my narrative of the events which have taken place since I left Jerusalem. The God of our father Abraham be your defence and shield.

Your affectionate daughter,

Adina.

LETTER VIII.

My Dear Father:

My last letter ended with an account of the Roman escort, under the authority of the young Roman centurion who, as I have before written to you, with so much courtesy proffered its protection to our little party. The day was yet early, and the air was of that buoyant elasticity so agreeable to breathe, and which strikes me as one of the peculiar blessings of this holy land of our fathers. As I rode along, I felt as if I would gladly mount the Arabian of the desert and fly across the sandy seas of Edom, with the fleetness which amazes me whenever I see the children of the desert ride; for a band of thirty came boldly near us from a gorge as we approached Bethany, and after watching us a few moments, scoured away into the recesses of the hills like the wind, as a detachment of our Roman escort was ordered to gallop towards them. We were fortunate in having such strong protection.

We soon afterwards reached the summit of the ridge above Bethany, from which eminence we had a gorgeous view of the Holy City of God, with its lofty Temple glittering in the sunbeams. The Tower of Antonia darkly contrasted with its splendor, and the citadel of David frowned over the walls with a warlike majesty that deeply impressed me. I drew rein, and entreated Rabbi Amos to delay a few moments while I surveyed Jerusalem, but he was too far ahead to hear me, and the centurion, riding up to my side, stopped respectfully with a portion of his command, and said he would await my leisure. I could not but thank him for his civility, and then turning towards the city, I was soon lost to all else but the awful contemplation of it.

"You should see Rome," said the centurion, who had watched my emotion evidently with surprise. "It is a city of grandeur unequalled. It covers six times more space than this city, and it contains three hundred and sixty-five temples, while Jerusalem contains but one!"

"There is no God but one," I answered, impressively.

"We believe there is one God, who is the author of a great multitude of lesser gods, and to each we erect a temple," he said firmly, yet respectfully.

Rome

Upon this, touched with pity that one so noble in mind and person should be so ignorant of the truth, I began to show him from the Prophets that God was one, and that all things were made by him. But he, plucking a blossom from a tree within reach, said:

"It is beneath the dignity of the Father of the gods, the great Jove, to descend to make a flower like this, or shape a crystal, or color the ruby, or create that golden-eyed humming-bird which flutters among those fragrant blossoms. He made the sun, and moon, and stars, and earth, but left the lesser works to inferior deities. Talk to me of thy one God, and prove to me, maiden, that he made all things, and is one, and thy God shall be my God."

We now rode forward through the street of Bethany, and soon came to the house of our former friend, Rabbi Abel, who died many years ago at Alexandria, when he went there with merchandise, and after the welfare of whose children you desired me to make inquiries. It was a plain and humble dwelling before which Rabbi Amos assisted me to alight; but there was an air of neatness and sweet domestic repose about it that at once came home to my heart, and made me love the place even before I had seen the inmates. On hearing of my arrival, there came out a fair young girl of twenty-two, with the most amiable expression of affectionate welcome, and approaching me with mingled respect and love, she embraced me, while Rabbi Amos pronounced our names to each other. I felt immediately as if I were in a sister's arms, and that I should love her always. Next came forth a young man of about thirty years of age, with a countenance of an exceedingly interesting expression, full of intellect and good will. He was pale and habitually thoughtful, but a fine friendly light beamed in his dark, handsome eyes, as he extended his hand to welcome me. You have already had a full description of him, and of his character, in one of my former letters, and need not be told that it was Lazarus, the son of your friend. At the threshold Martha, the eldest sister, met me, but with more ceremony, and made an apology for receiving me, the rich heiress of Alexandria, as she termed me, into so lowly a dwelling; but I embraced her so affectionately that this feeling passed away instantly. Martha busied herself at once to prepare refreshments for us, and soon set before us a frugal but agreeable repast. Mary, in the meanwhile, and Lazarus, sat on either side of me, and asked me many questions about Alexandria.

I cannot describe to you the loveliness of the person of Mary, and yet not so much the perfection of features as the soul which animates them, and lends them a charm that I cannot adequately convey to you.

Martha, the oldest, is of a more lively disposition, yet more commanding in her aspect, being taller and almost queenly in her mien. Her eyes and her hair are jet black; the former mild and beaming with intelligence, like those of her brother Lazarus, whom she resembles. She has a winning voice, and a manner that leads you to feel strong confidence in her friendship. She seemed to take the whole management of our entertainment upon herself. Lazarus conversed chiefly with Rabbi Amos, who questioned him with much interest about the prophet John of the wilderness. After our repast, Martha showed me three beautiful bands of embroidery, which she was working for the new vail of the Temple to be put on next year; for the sisters live by working needle-work for the Temple, and Lazarus makes copies of the Laws and Psalms for the priests. He showed me his copying-table, and the rolls of parchment upon it, some partly inscribed in beautiful characters, some quite complete. He also showed me a copy of the book of Isaiah, which had occupied him one hundred and seven days. It was exquisitely executed.

Seeing upon the table a richly worked book-cover of silk and velvet, with the letters, "J. N." embroidered in olive leaves upon it, I asked Mary if that, being so elegant, was not for the High Priest.

"No," answered Martha, with brightening eyes, speaking before her sister could reply, "that is for our friend, and the friend and brother of Lazarus."

"What is his name?" I asked.

"Jesus, of Nazareth."

"I have heard John speak of this person," said my cousin Mary, with animation. "I should feel happy to know him also."

"If you had been here a few days ago," replied Martha, "you would have seen him. He left us, after being with us three weeks, to return to Nazareth. But he requested to meet Lazarus at Bethabara, on the third day from this, for some important reason; and my brother will go, for he loves him so that he would cross the seas to meet him."

"Then," said Rabbi Amos to Lazarus, "if you are to journey so soon towards Jordan to meet your friend, you had best join our company and share our escort." To this Lazarus consented.

I left this blessed abode with regret, and felt that I should be perfectly happy if I could be admitted as a fifth link in the wealth of their mutual love.

About noon we stopped at a caravanserai, half the way to Jericho from Bethany. Here we overtook a friend of Rabbi Amos, the venerable and learned scholar and lawyer, Gamaliel. Accompanying the lawyer, Gamaliel, was a young man who was his disciple, and who went with him as a companion by the way. His name is Saul, and I noticed him particularly, because I overheard the venerable lawyer say that he was the most remarkable young man who had ever sat at his feet to learn the mysteries of the law. This young law disciple and Lazarus rode together, and talked long and earnestly by the way, the former thinking that nothing but mischief would come of the new prophet's preaching, while the latter warmly defended him and his mission as divine. To their conversation the Roman centurion listened with the closest attention, for Saul was learned in the Prophets, and drew richly from its stores to prove that the true Messias can never be heralded by so mean a messenger as this preacher of repentance in the wilderness.

I now write to thee beneath the roof of the country residence of Rabbi Amos. To-morrow early we are going to Bethabara, a little village beyond Jordan, but situated on its banks, near which we learn John is now baptizing. Lazarus has gone on with Saul and the learned Gamaliel, with many lawyers and doctors in company, who desire to see and hear this prophet of the wilderness.

That the hope of Israel may not be long deferred, and that we may receive the Messias, when he cometh, in humble faith, in honor and in love, is the prayer of

Your affectionate daughter,

Adina.

LETTER IX.

My Dear Father:

In these letters to you I hope you will pardon the details which I enter into, for it is my earnest desire that you should see everything with my eyes, as if you had been present with me, in order that you may be able to judge of the remarkable events of which I have undertaken to give you a complete history.

After Rabbi Amos had reached the house in the wheat fields of Gilgal, he kindly told us that he was ready to accompany my cousin Mary and myself to the Jordan to hear the prophet. We had not ridden a great way from the house when we overtook two men on foot, with staves in their hands and wallets upon their shoulders. As we passed, one of them bowed with respect to Rabbi Amos, who, from his rank as a priest and his venerable appearance, always commands the homage of all men.

"Whither goest thou at such a pace, friend Matthew?" said Rabbi Amos, returning his salutation. "Canst thou leave thy tax-gathering these busy times to go into the wilderness?"

The person, who was a man of stout figure, with dark hair and beard and a look of intelligence, but whose costume was plain and ill-worn, smiled and answered:

"If a man would find the payers of tribute nowadays, good master, he must not stay at home, forsooth, but go into the wilderness of Jordan. Verily, this new prophet emptieth our towns, and we publicans must remain idle in our seat of customs or go with the tide."

"And thinkest thou," continued my uncle, as the two men walked along by the side of his mule, "thinkest thou this prophet is a true son of the prophets?"

"He works no miracles, unless indeed the power of his preaching be a miracle," answered Matthew.

"This man is an impostor. There can be no prophet unless he prove his mission by miracles," suddenly said the companion of Matthew, speaking up abruptly in a sharp and unpleasing voice. Now neither Mary nor I liked the face of this man from the first. He was low in height, was ill-featured, and his attire was mean; but he had a suspicious air, combined with a cringing deference to Rabbi Amos, that made me think he must be a hypocrite. He smiled with his mouth and teeth, but at the same time looked sinister out of his eyes. An air of humility seemed to me to be put on to conceal the pride and wickedness of his character. He looked like a man who could artfully deceive to gain his selfish ends, and who would kneel to you to overturn you. The sound of his voice confirmed my first impression of him. Upon speaking, Rabbi Amos fixed his eyes upon him, as if he did not like the manner of his breaking in upon the conversation.

"What is thy companion's name, friend Matthew?" he asked aside, as the other walked on ahead.

"His name is Judas, called Iscariot. He hath been engaged by me to bear the moneys I collect in the country villages; and as we are to gather taxes both at Gilgal and Bethabara, he cometh with me."

At length, dear father, after hastening the speed of our mules and riding pleasantly for two hours along the verdant banks of Jordan, we came in sight of a square tower of stone, peering above the trees which marked the site of the village of Bethabara. "That tower," said Rabbi Amos, "stands over a cave in which Elijah long dwelt. From the summit of yonder hill, at the left, the prophet was caught up and ascended to heaven upon the chariot of fire; and near where you see the single rock, Elisha divided Jordan with the fallen mantle left him by the ascending prophet of God."

While my eyes were fixed upon the hill, and my imagination presented to me Elijah standing upon the chariot of heaven, disappearing amid the clouds, there was an opening in the wood before us, and all at once we beheld a scene that made my heart cease to beat, it was so new and wonderful. Near the place the winding river takes a broad curve, and the opposite village of Bethabara lies in the hollow of it, forming the center of half a circle. This widely curving shore was alive with the human heads that filled it. And of this vast multitude every eye was concentrated upon the prophet. He was standing near the opposite shore (the Jordan here is very narrow and can be forded), in the water, addressing the countless assembly that stood opposite to and half encircling him. Near him, behind, and on either side, sat his disciples, upon the bank, at least a hundred in number, chiefly young men.

The clear voice of the youthful prophet of the wilderness fell distinctly on our ears, so great was the stillness of the vast audience. To my surprise I saw John, the cousin of Mary, standing close to the prophet, and listening with the deepest and most reverent attention to every syllable he uttered. The subject of the prophet's discourse was as before, and as always, the coming of the Messias. Oh, that I could give you, my dear father, the faintest idea of the power and eloquence of his language!

"Do you ask me if the blood of bulls and goats take not away sin? I answer and say unto you, that the Lord hath said that he delighteth not in these rivers of blood," he continued earnestly.

"For what, then, great prophet," asked one of the chief Levites, who stood near him, "for what, then, are the sacrifices ordained by the law of Moses? for what then the altar in the Temple, and the daily sacrifice of the lamb?"

"For what?" repeated the prophet, with his eyes beaming with the earnest light of inspiration; "for what but as types and shadows of the real and true sacrifice appointed by God from the foundation of the world? Think ye a man can give the lamb of his flock for himself? Nay, men of Israel, the day has come when your eyes shall be opened. The hour is at hand when the true meaning of the daily sacrifice shall be understood. Lo, the Messiah cometh, and ye shall see and believe!"

There now came several persons towards him who desired baptism. While he was baptizing these persons, both men and women, I saw appear on a little mound near the tower, Lazarus, the brother of Martha, accompanied by a man of about his own years, of an indescribable dignity and grace of aspect, combined with an air of benevolence and peace that at once attracted me.

He was wrapped in a vesture of dark blue cloth, which was folded about his form; his head was bare, and his hair flowed like a Nazarene's down about his shoulders. He seemed so unlike all other men, in a certain majesty united with sweetness that marked his whole air, that I could not withdraw my gaze from him.

The prophet at the same moment rested his eyes upon him, and as he did so, I saw a change come over his face, as if he had seen an angel. His eyes shone with unearthly brilliancy; his lips parted as if he would speak, yet had lost the power; and then, with his right hand stretched forth towards the noble stranger, he stood for a moment like a statue. All eyes followed his and the direction of his stretched-out arm. Suddenly he exclaimed, and oh, how like the trumpet of Horeb his voice rang!—

"Behold!"

There was not a face in that vast multitude that was not directed towards the little eminence.

"Ye have asked wherefore is slain the daily lamb," continued the prophet. "The day has come when the lamb of sacrifice, which can take away no sin, shall cease. Behold!" And here he stretched forth both arms towards the dignified stranger. "Behold him who taketh away the transgressions of men! He it is who, coming after me, is preferred before me. He it is to whom I bear witness, as the Messiah, the Son of the Highest! There stands the Christ of God! the only true Lamb, whose blood can take away the iniquities of us all. He hath dwelt among you, he hath walked your streets, he hath sat in your homes, and I knew him not, till I now behold on him the sign of the Messiah!"

When the prophet had thus spoken in a voice that thrilled to every bosom, we beheld the august stranger advance towards the prophet. He moved on alone. Lazarus had fallen prostrate on his face. As he continued to come forward, all was expectation in the immense multitude. The mass of heads swayed this way and that, to get a sight of his face, which I could see was serene, but pale and earnest. John, the cousin of Mary, seeing him approach, lowly knelt, and bowed his head in reverential awe and love. Those who stood between him and the prophet moved involuntarily apart, and left an open path for him to the water-side. He walked at a slow and even pace, with an air of humility veiling the native dignity of his kingly port.

The prophet, on seeing him come near, regarded him, as it seemed to me, with far more awe than all others.

"What wouldst thou of thy servant, O Messiah, Prophet of God, mighty to save?" he said, in tremulous tones, as the stranger came even some paces into the water towards him.

"To be baptized of thee," answered the Christ, in a still, quiet voice, that was heard to the remotest bounds of the crowd. Never, oh, never shall I forget the sounds of that voice, as it fell upon my ears!

"I have need to be baptized of thee; and comest thou to me?" answered the prophet, with the lowliest humility and awe of manner and with looks expressive of his amazement.

"It becometh us to fulfill all righteousness," answered Messiah, mildly; and when he had said this, the prophet, though still with a manner of doubt, and with the holiest reverence, administered then unto him, in the sight of all the people, the like baptism which he had administered to his disciples.

And now, my dear father, comes to be related the most extraordinary thing that ever took place in Israel since the Law was given from Sinai.

No sooner did the baptized stranger go up out of the water, than there was heard above all our heads a noise as of rolling thunder, although the sky was cloudless; and when in great fear we looked up, we beheld a dazzling glory far brighter than the sun, and from the midst of this celestial splendor there darted with arrowy velocity a ray of light which descended and lit upon the head of the Christ. Some of the people said it thundered, and others that it lightened, but judge of the amazement and admiration of all, and the dread awe that shook every soul when, amid the glory above his head, was seen the form of a dove of fire, with outspread wings overshadowing him as it were, and from the heavens what was supposed to be thunder shaped itself into a voice, which uttered these words in the hearing of every ear:

"This is my beloved Son, in whom I am well pleased!"

At hearing these words from the skies a great part of the multitude fell on their faces. Every cheek was pale, and each man gazed on his neighbor in wonder and fear. When the majestic, yet terrible, voice had given utterance to these words, the light disappeared, the dove re-ascended to the skies and was lost to sight, leaving a halo of divine glory resting upon the head of this "Son of God." He alone seemed unmoved and calm amid all this awful scene, and going up the river bank, disappeared mysteriously and suddenly from my earnest gaze. At length, when men came a little to themselves, and would gaze on him whom all knew now to be the Christ, no one could find him, so effectually had he withdrawn himself from their homage.

Your affectionate,

Adina.

LETTER X.

My Dear Father:

I shall now resume the narrative interrupted by the close of my last letter.

The excitement which the sudden disappearance of Jesus produced, led to a universal separation of the multitude. No one knew whence he had gone save John, Mary's cousin, and Lazarus, who reverently followed him. The prophet John, of Jordan, appeared to me to be more surprised at what had taken place than any others. He looked constantly around for Jesus, and then, with his hands clasped together and uplifted, gazed heavenward, as if satisfied, with the thousands around him, that He had been received up into heaven.

Rabbi Amos and our party remained standing near the water, for he desired to speak with John, who stood alone in the midst of the water, precisely where he had baptized Jesus. Not one of his disciples remained with him. Rabbi Amos drew near, and said to him:

"Holy prophet, knowest thou what man, if man he may be called, was just baptized by thee?"

The prophet, whose eyes had been steadfastly raised all the while, bent his looks with tearful tenderness upon Rabbi Amos, and said, plaintively and touchingly:

"This is he of whom I spake, After me cometh a man which is preferred before me, for he was before me. And I knew him not; but he that sent me to baptize with water, the same said unto me, Upon whom thou shalt see the Spirit descending and remaining on him, the same is he that baptizeth with the Holy Ghost. And I saw the Spirit descending like a dove; and I saw and bear record that this is the Son of God."

"And whither, oh, holy prophet of Jordan," asked Rabbi Amos, with deep and sacred interest, "whither has he departed?"

"That I know not. He must increase and I must decrease, whether he remaineth on earth or has been taken up into heaven. My mission is now drawing to its close, for he to whom I have borne witness is come."

Thus speaking, he turned and walked out of the water on the side towards Bethabara, and disappeared among the trees that fringed the bank. I now looked in the face of Rabbi Amos, upon whose arm Mary was tearfully leaning. His face was grave and thoughtful. I said, "Uncle, dost thou believe all that thou hast seen and heard?"

"I know not what to say," he answered, "only that the things which I have beheld this day are evidences that God has not forgotten his people Israel." He said no more. We left the banks of the Jordan in silence and awe, and remounting our mules, returned towards my uncle's house at Gilgal. On the way we constantly passed crowds of people, all in high talk about the wonderful events which had taken place at the river. The impression seemed universally to be that Jesus had gone up into heaven after he was baptized.

But, my dear father, it is with deep joy that I am able to tell you that this wonderful person is still on the earth. I stated that my cousin John and Lazarus had kept their eyes upon him from the first, and that they had seen him pass down the river, where some projecting and overhanging trees hid him at once from view. Though they often lost sight of him, they yet followed him by the print of his sandals in the wet sand of the shore, and at length came in view of him, as he was leaving the river bank, and going towards the desert, between two low hills, which hid him from their eyes.

They went on, but though they moved forward rapidly, they next saw him far distant, crossing the arid plain that stretches south towards Jericho and the desert. They ran very swiftly, and at length coming near him, called, "Master, good master, stay for us, for we would follow and learn of thee!"

He stopped, and turned upon them a visage so pale and marred with sadness and anguish, that they both stood still and gazed upon him with amazement at beholding such a change. The glory of his beauty had passed away, and the beaming splendor which shone upon his countenance was wholly gone. The expression of unutterable sorrow that remained pierced them to the heart. Lazarus, who had been so long his bosom friend, wept aloud. "Weep not! thou shalt see me another day, my friends," he said. "I now go to the wilderness, in obedience to the Spirit which guideth me thither. Thou shalt, after a time, behold me again. It is expedient for you that I go whither I go."

"Nay, but we will go with thee," said Lazarus, earnestly. "If thou art to endure evil, we will be with thee."

"There must be none to help. There must be none to uphold," he said firmly, but sadly. "I must tread the winepress of temptation alone!"

He then left them, waving his hand for them to go back. They obeyed sorrowfully, wondering what his words meant, and wherefore it was needful for him to go into the desert, where certain mysterious trials seemed to wait for him; and they wondered most of all at the change in his countenance, which, from being lustrous with celestial light, was now, said Lazarus, "marred more than the sons of men." From time to time the two young men looked backward to watch the receding figure of the Christ, till they no longer distinguished him in the distance of the desert, towards the dreadful solitudes of which he steadfastly kept his face.

The two friends came on to the house of Rabbi Amos, at Gilgal, the same night, and we sat together late at night upon the porch under the fig trees, talking of Jesus.

Now, my dear father, how wonderful is all this! That a great Prophet is among us, cannot be denied. The star of John the Baptizer's fame dwindles into a glow-worm before the glory of this Son of God! That he will draw all men unto him, even into the wilderness, if he takes up his abode there, cannot be questioned. But all is mystery, awe, curiosity, wonder, and excitement just now.

May the God of our fathers' house come forth indeed from the heavens, for the salvation of his people!

Your devoted and loving,

Adina.

LETTER XI.

My Dear Father:

In my last letter to you I spoke of our return from Jordan to Gilgal. At the house were assembled not only John, the cousin of Mary, and the noble Lazarus, but also Gamaliel and Saul. The court of the dwelling was thronged with strangers, and the common people who, being far from their homes and without food, had freely been invited to lodgings and food by the hospitable priest.

As we sat up late conversing with deep interest upon the remarkable events of the day, an observation made by John, when speaking of the change in the face of Jesus, that "His face was marred more than the sons of men," led the venerable Gamaliel to say to us:

"Those are the words of the prophet Esaias, and are truly spoken by him of Messias, when he shall come."

"Let us consult Esaias, then, and see what further he hath said," cried Rabbi Amos. "Mary, bring hither the roll of the Prophets."

My Cousin Mary returned, and placed the book on a small stand before him.

"Read aloud, worthy Rabbi," said the philosopher Gamaliel, "we will all listen; for though I do not believe this young man who was to-day baptized is Messias and the Christ, who is to restore all things to us, yet I am prepared to reverence him as a great prophet."

"And," answered Rabbi Amos, "if we find the prophecies do meet in him that which we look for to meet in Messias when he cometh, wilt thou believe, venerable father?"

"I will believe and reverently adore," answered the sage, bowing his head till his flowing white beard almost touched his knees.

"Read Adina, for thy eyes are young," said my uncle; and I read as follows:

"'Behold, my Servant shall deal prudently, he shall be exalted and extolled, and be very high. As many were astonished at thee; his visage was so marred more than any man, and his form more than the sons of men.'"

"How completely," said John, "those words describe his appearance on the verge of the desert, and yet I used them unconsciously."

"But," said Saul, Gamaliel's disciple, "if this be prophesied of the Christ, then we are to have a Christ of humiliation, and not one of honor and glory. Read one part which you have omitted, maiden."

I read on as follows: "'Behold, my Servant shall be exalted and extolled, and be very high. He shall sprinkle many nations; the kings shall shut their mouths at him. He shall lift up his hand to the Gentiles, and set up his standard to the people. Kings shall bow down to him with their faces to the earth, and lick up the dust of his feet!'"

"There! Such is our Messias!" exclaimed Saul.

"Yes, it is a Christ of power and dominion who is to redeem Israel," added Gamaliel; "not an unknown young man, scarcely thirty years of age, who came from whence no one knoweth, and hath gone as he came. As for the Christ, we shall know whence he cometh!"

At hearing this great and good man thus discourse, dear father, my heart sank within me, for Lazarus had already told us that his friend Jesus was of humble birth, a carpenter's son, and his mother a widow; that he had known him from boyhood, but known him only to love him. I now looked towards him, but I took courage when I saw that the words of Gamaliel did not in the least dim the light of faith and confidence which brightly sparkled in his eyes, that his friend Jesus was truly Messias of God. But my eye fell on what follows, and as I read it I gained more confidence: "He hath no form nor comeliness; and when we shall see him there is no beauty that we should desire him."

"If the first part of this prophecy," said Lazarus, his fine eyes lighting up, as he looked at Saul, "be of the Christ, as you have just now confessed, then is this last of him; and the fact that you reject him is but the fulfillment of this part of the prophecy."

Hereupon arose a very warm discussion between Gamaliel and Saul on one side, and Rabbi Amos, John and Lazarus on the other.

"But let this be as it may," said John, after the arguments on both sides had been mainly exhausted, "how will you, O Gamaliel, and you, Saul, get over the extraordinary voice and fiery appearance which distinguished the baptism?"

"That must have been a phenomenon of nature, or done by the art of the famed Babylonish sorcerer, whom I saw prominent in the multitude," answered the philosopher.

"Did you not hear the words?" asked Rabbi Amos.

"Yes, Rabbi; nevertheless, they may have been thrown into the air from the lungs of this sorcerer; for they do marvelous things."

"Would you suppose that a sorcerer would be disposed to apply the sacred words of the Lord?" asked John, earnestly.

"By no means," he answered, reverently.

"If Rabbi Amos will allow me, I will show you the very words in King David's prophecies of Messias."

All looked with interest on John, as he took from his mantle a roll of the Psalms. He opened it and read as follows:

"'Why do the rulers take counsel together against the Lord, and against his Anointed? I will declare the decree. The Lord hath said unto me, Thou art my Son.'"

Upon hearing this read, Gamaliel was thoughtful.

"It is extraordinary," answered he. "I will search the Scriptures when I reach Jerusalem, to see if these things be so."

"But," said Saul, with some vehemence, "listen while I read some prophecies also." And he unrolled the book of the Prophets and read these words:

"'Thou, Bethlehem Ephratah, though thou be little among the thousands of Judah, yet out of thee shall he come forth unto me that is to be ruler in Israel, whose goings forth have been from of old, from everlasting.'

"Now, you will confess, Rabbi Amos," he added, with a look of triumph, "that this word refers to our expected Messias?"

"Without doubt," answered my uncle, "but—"

"Wait, I beseech you, learned Rabbi," said Saul, "until I read you another prophecy." And he read: "'I have made a covenant with David, Thy seed will I establish forever, and build up thy throne to all generations. His seed shall endure forever, and his throne as the sun before me. Behold, the days come, saith the Lord, that I will raise unto David a righteous Branch.'

"Now, you will all admit, brethren, that these prophecies refer to Messias. He is therefore to come of the lineage of David, and he is to be born in Bethlehem. Show me that this Jesus, the Nazarene, fulfills both conditions in his own person, and I will prepare to believe in him."

This was said haughtily, and with the air of one who cannot be answered.

But immediately Lazarus rose to his feet and said: "Although I did not recollect this prophecy, that Christ was to be born in Bethlehem, yet I am overjoyed to find the fact respecting Jesus fulfills it. He was born in Bethlehem of Judah. This I have known some years, and—"

Here, while my heart was bounding with joy, Gamaliel said sternly, "I thought this man was born in Nazareth?"

"He has lived," answered Lazarus, "in Nazareth from childhood only. During the days when Cæsar Augustus issued a decree that all the world should be taxed, his mother, and Joseph her husband, went up to the City of David to be taxed, which is Bethlehem, and there Jesus was born, as I have often heard from her lips."

"Admitting, then, that he was born in Bethlehem," said Saul, "you have to prove his lineage from David's line."

"Wherefore did his parents go to Bethlehem, David's city, unless they were of his royal line?" asked Rabbi Amos, "for none went to any other city to be taxed than that of their own family. The fact that they went there is strong evidence that they were of David's house."

"Every one born in the city of David," remarked Gamaliel, "is not of necessity of David's house; but it is surprising if this Jesus really was born in Bethlehem."

"But may not his lineage be ascertained without a doubt from the records of the tribes, and of their families, kept by command of the law of the Temple?" I asked of my uncle.

"Without question. These books of the generations of our people are to be relied on," he answered.

"In fact," said Gamaliel, "they are kept with the greatest accuracy, and it is so ordained by God, for the very reason that when Messias cometh we may know whether he who claims to be such be of the house of David or no. I will examine the book of the generations, and see if his mother and father come of the stock and seed of David."

"And if you find that they do," asked John, with emotion, "can you doubt any longer whether Jesus be the Christ? Will not the fact of his being born in Bethlehem, and of the lineage of David, not to speak of the witness of God's own audible voice, heard by our ears this day, will not these facts lead you to believe that he is the Christ?"

"They will prevent me from actually rejecting him," answered the cold philosopher. "But every child born in Bethlehem, and of the house of David, and there are many of them in Judah, fulfills, so far, the conditions of these two prophecies; these are not, therefore, Messiahs."

"What more can you ask for?" asked Mary, with feeling, for she strongly believed that Jesus was the Christ.

"Miracles," answered the disciple of Gamaliel, glancing at the face of his master inquiringly.

"Yes, miracles," also answered the sage. "The Messiah is to heal the sick by a word, restore sight to the blind, cast out devils, and even raise the dead."

"If he restore the blind and raise the dead, I will doubt no longer," answered Saul.

There was at this moment an interruption caused by noisy altercations in the court among some of John the Baptist's disciples. Rabbi Amos, as host, went out to put an end to these disputings, when Gamaliel retired to his chamber, and the conversation was not renewed.

Your daughter,

Adina.

LETTER XII.

My Dear Father:

Let me resume the interesting subject of which my letters have been so full.

It is now eight weeks since our return from Gilgal. For five weeks after we reached Jerusalem, we heard nothing of Jesus, until John, son of Elisaph, reappeared. He and Lazarus came into the city together, and to the house of Rabbi Amos. Our first inquiry was:

"Have you seen him? Have you heard anything from him?"

"John has seen him," answered Lazarus, seriously. "Ask him, and he will tell you all."

We looked at John, who sat sad and pensive, as if he were dwelling in his mind upon some painful, yet tender, sorrow. The eyes of my Cousin Mary, which always caught their lustre from his, were shaded with an inquiring look of sympathy and solicitude.

"You are not well, I fear," she said, placing her fair hand upon his white brow, and putting back the hair from his temples. "You have been long away, and are weary and ill."

"Weary, Mary? I shall never complain of weariness again, after what I have beheld."

"What have you seen?" I asked.

"Jesus in the desert; and when I remember him there, I shall forget to smile more."

"You have found him, then?" I eagerly asked.

"Yes, after days of painful search. I found him in the very center of the Desert of Ashes, where foot of man had never trodden before. I saw him upon his knees, and heard his voice in prayer. I laid down the sack of bread and fishes and the skin of water I had brought with me to succor him, and with awe drew near where he stood.

"As I came closer to him, I heard him groan in spirit, and he seemed to be borne down to the earth by some mortal agony. He was, as it were, talking to some invisible evil beings who assailed him.

"'Rabbi, good Master,' I said, 'I have brought thee food and water. Pardon me if I have intruded upon thy awful loneliness, which is sacred to some deep grief; but I weep with thee for thy woes, and in all thy afflictions I am afflicted. Eat, that thou mayest have strength to endure thy mysterious sufferings.'

"He turned his pale countenance full upon me, and extended towards me his emaciated hands, while he smiled faintly, and blessed me and said:

"'Son, thou art very dear to me. Thou shalt one day be afflicted for me, but not now, and then understand wherefore I am now a sufferer in the desert.'

"'Let me remain with thee, Divine Messias,' I said.

"'Thou believest, then, that I am he?' he answered, regarding me with love.

"I replied by casting myself at his desert-parched feet, and bathing them with my tears. He raised me and said, 'Go thy way presently. When the time of my fasting and temptation is past, I will see thee again.'

"'Nay, I will not leave thee,' I asserted.

"'If thou lovest me, beloved, thou wilt obey me,' he answered, with a tone of gentle reproof.

"'But thou wilt first eat of the bread I have brought, and drink of the water,' I entreated.

"'Thou knowest not what temptation thou art offering to me,' he replied, sadly. 'Thou hast not enough for thine own needs. Go, and leave me to gain the victory over Satan, the prince of this world, for which I was led by the Spirit thither.'

"I once more cast myself at his feet, and he lifted me up, kissing me, and sent me away. Oh, you would not have known him! Worn and emaciated by long abstinence, weak through suffering, he looked but the shadow of himself. He could not have lived thus if there had not been a divine power within to sustain him! His existence so long, for he had been in the desert five weeks without food when I found him, was a miracle in itself, proving the power of God to be in him."

"For what mighty work among men is God preparing him?" said Rabbi Amos, with emotion. "Surely he is a prophet come from God."

"Think you he still lives?" I asked, with anxious fears, scarcely trusting my voice above a whisper.

"Yes," answered John. "I am come to tell you he was divinely sustained through all; and after forty days he came forth from the wilderness, and suddenly presented himself on the banks of Jordan, among John's disciples. I was standing near the Baptizer, discoursing of the Christ, and marvelling when his exile to the desert would terminate, when the prophet, lifting his eyes, cried with a loud voice full of joy:

"'Behold again the Lamb of God, upon whom the Spirit of God descended! He hath come from the furnace like gold seven times tried in the fire! He it is who alone taketh away the sins of the world!'

"I turned and beheld Jesus advancing. He was pale and wore an expression of gentle, uncomplaining suffering on his benign and spiritualized countenance. I hastened to meet him, and was kneeling in joy at his feet, when he embraced me as a brother and said, 'Faithful, and full of love, wilt thou follow me?'

"'I will nevermore leave thee,' I answered.

"'Where dwellest thou, divine Master?' then asked one of John's disciples, Andrew by name, who was with me.

"'Come, my friends, and see,' he answered; and we went after him with joy unutterable.

"He entered the village of Bethabara, and, approaching the house of a widow, where he abode, went in. We followed him, and by his request took up our abode with him. Oh, how shall I be able to make known by words," added John, "the sweet expression of his discourse! In one day in his presence I grew wise; his words filled the soul like new wine and made the heart glad. The next day he wished to go into Galilee, and so on to Nazareth, where his mother dwelleth; and as I have made up my mind to follow him as his disciple henceforth, I have only come hither to make known my purpose to Mary, and to arrange my affairs in the city. To-morrow I will leave again, to join this, my dear Lord, at Cana of Galilee."

"Canst thou divine at all his purpose?" asked Rabbi Amos of John, "whether he intends to found a school of wisdom, to preach like the prophets, to reign like David, or to conquer like his warrior namesake, Joshua?"

"I know not, save that he said he came to redeem that which was lost, and to establish a kingdom that shall have no end."

Upon hearing this, all our hearts bounded with hope and confidence in him, and we all together burst forth into a voice of thanksgiving, and sang this hymn of praise:

> "O sing unto the Lord a new song. He hath done marvelous things; his right hand and his holy arm hath gotten the victory.

"The Lord hath made known his salvation; his righteousness hath he openly shewed in the sight of the heathen.

"He hath remembered his mercy and his truth towards the house of Israel; all the ends of the earth have seen the salvation of our God."

There was this morning, dear father, no little excitement produced among the chief priests by a formal inquiry sent by Pilate to Caiaphas, the High Priest, asking whether this new prophet was to be acknowledged by them as their Messiah, "for, if he is to be, it will be my duty," said the Governor, "to place him under arrest, inasmuch as we understand the Jewish Messias is to declare himself king." Upon this there was a tumultuous assembling together of the priests in the porch of the Temple, and with many invectives they agreed to send answer to Pilate that they did not acknowledge Jesus of Nazareth to be the Christ. What Pilate will conclude to do, I know not. Rabbi Amos informed us that the Procurator had got some news by courier that morning that Jesus, on his way to Cana, had been followed by a full thousand people, who hailed him as the Christ.

Thus you see, my dear father, that this divine person is already taking hold of the hearts of the people, and arousing the jealousy of our enemies. Be assured that the day will come when he will lift up his standard to the Gentiles, and draw all men unto him.

Your loving,

Adina.

LETTER XIII.

My Dear Father:

Since I last wrote you, my faith has been confirmed by the testimony which in one of your letters you demanded. You said, "Let me hear that he has done an authentic miracle in attestation of the divinity of his mission—such a miracle as was prophesied Messias shall do, as healing the sick by a word, restoring the blind to sight, and raising the dead—and I will prepare to believe in him."

Miracle he has performed, dear father, and one the genuineness of which is not disputed by any one. I can give you the particulars best by extracting from a letter written by John to Mary, a few days after his departure to join Jesus at Nazareth:

"Upon reaching Nazareth," says the letter, "I was guided to the humble dwelling occupied by the mother of Jesus, by a large concourse of people gathered about it, of whom inquiring, I learned that it was to see the new Prophet they had thus assembled. 'What new Prophet?' I asked, wishing to know what the multitude thought of Jesus.

"'The one of whom John of the wilderness foretold,' answered one.

"'They say he is Messias,' replied another.

"'He is the Christ,' boldly asserted a third.

"Hereupon a Levite standing by, said scornfully, 'Does Christ come out of the country of Galilee? You read the Prophets to little purpose, if you see therein any Christ prophesied to come out of Nazareth of Galilee.' Hereupon, seeing the faith of many staggered, I said, 'Brethren, Christ is truly to be of Bethlehem, and verily Jesus, though now he dwelleth in this place, was born in Bethlehem.'

"'Thou canst not prove it, man!' said the Levite angrily.

"'The stranger speaketh truly,' spoke up both an old man and a gray-haired woman in the crowd. 'We know that he was not born here, and that when his parents moved hither, when he was an infant, they then said he was born in Bethlehem. We all remember this well.'

"Hereupon the Levite, seeing that he had not the people with him, passed on his way, while I went to the door of the house where Jesus dwelt with his mother. There were two doors, one of which led into a workshop, where I noticed the bench and tools of the occupation at which he had toiled to support himself and his mother. But when, as I entered the dwelling, I saw him standing, teaching those who hung on his lips, and listened to his calm voice, and heard the sublime wisdom of his instructions, beheld the dignity of his aspect, and felt the heavenly benignity of his manner, I forgot the carpenter, I forgot the man, and seemed to behold in him only Messiah the Prince, the Son of God.

"Upon beholding me, he extended his hand, and received me graciously, and said, pointing to five men who stood near him, regarding him with mingled love and reverence, 'These are thy brethren, who have also come out of the world to follow me.'

"Of these, one was Andrew, who had been, as well as myself, John's disciple. Another was Andrew's brother, whose name is Simon, whom Jesus, from the firmness and immovable zeal of his character, which he seemed to understand, called also Peter, or Stone. The fourth disciple was of Bethsaida. His name was Philip, and he followed Jesus from having been prepared by John the Baptist to receive him. He was, moreover, so overjoyed at finding the Christ, that he ran to the house of his kinsman, Nathaniel, and finding him in his garden, beneath a fig tree, at prayer, exclaimed:

"'We have found him of whom Moses in the law and the prophets did write, the Messias of God!'

"'Where is he, that I may behold him?' asked his relative, rising.

"'It is Jesus of Nazareth, the son of Joseph,' Philip answered.

"Upon hearing this answer, the countenance of Nathaniel fell, and he replied:

"'Can there any good thing come out of Nazareth?'

"'Come thou and see for thyself,' answered Philip.

"Nathaniel then went with him where Jesus was. When Jesus saw him approaching, he said to those about him:

"'Behold an Israelite indeed, in whom there is no guile!'

"'Whence knowest thou me?' asked Nathaniel, with surprise, for he had heard the words which were spoken. Jesus answered and said:

"'Before Philip called thee, when thou wast under the fig tree, I saw thee.'

"Upon hearing this Nathaniel, who knew that he was all alone in his garden and unseen at prayer when his brother came, regarded the serene face of

Jesus steadfastly, and then, as if he beheld therein the expression of omnipresence, he cried before all the people:

"'Rabbi, thou art the Son of God! Thou art the King of Israel!'

"Jesus looked upon him as if pleased at his confession, and said:

"'Because I said unto thee, I saw thee under the fig tree, believest thou? Thou shalt see greater things than these. Verily, verily, I say unto you, hereafter ye shall see heaven open, and the angels of God ascending and descending upon the Son of man.'

"The next day James, my brother, and I went to the sea of Tiberias, but two hours distant, to see our father Zebedee, and transfer our interests to him; and, during the afternoon, Jesus passed near the shore on his way to Cana, when, calling us, we forever left our ships and our father and joined him. His mother and many of her kinsfolk were of the company, all going to a marriage of the cousin of the family. Upon our arrival at Cana, we were ushered into the guest chamber.

"The marriage feast at length commenced. The wine which should have come from Damascus had not arrived, the caravan having been delayed by the insurrection near Cesarea, and the chief ruler of the town, presiding at the feast, seeing that the wine had given out, bade the servants to place more upon the board. The mother of Jesus, who knew that the wine was out, and that, looking upon this as an ill omen, the family of the bride were in great distress, turned to Jesus and said, 'They have no wine.'

"The holy Prophet of God looked grave and said, applying to her the title which we deem most honorable of all others, 'Woman, what have I to do with thee? Mine hour is not yet come.'

"She must have understood his words, all mysterious as they were to me, for, turning to the servants, she beckoned to them, while her cheek borrowed a rich color from her hidden joy, and her eyes kindled with loving sympathy for those about to be relieved in their distress. When two or three of the servants had approached, she said to them:

"'Whatsoever he saith unto you, do it.'

"The face of Jesus, ever calm and dignified, now seemed to assume a look of majesty inexpressible, and his eyes to express a certain consciousness of power within, that awed me. Casting his glance upon several stone vases, which stood by the door empty, he said to the servants:

"'Fill the water pots with water.'

"In the court, in full sight from the table, was a well to which the servants forthwith went with jars, which I saw them fill with water, bear it in upon their heads, and pour it out into the water pots, until they had filled them all to the brim.

"In the meantime the governor of the feast and the majority of the guests were absorbed in conversation and did not observe what was taking place.

"'Draw out now and bear unto the governor of the feast,' said Jesus to the servants.

"They obeyed, and pouring rich, blood-red wine from the jars which I and others had seen filled up with simple water from the well, the amazed servants bore it to the chief of the feast. He had no sooner filled his goblet and tasted it, than he called to the bridegroom, who sat in the middle of the table, and said:

"'Every man at the beginning doth set forth good wine, and when men have well drunk, then that which is worse; but thou hast kept the good wine until now.'

"'Who hath brought this wine?' asked the bridegroom, drinking of the water that was made wine. 'Whence it came, sir, I know not.'

"Then the servants and others told that they had filled the six water pots with water to the brim, at the command of Jesus the Prophet, and that when they drew out, behold it flowed forth wine instead of water! Upon this there was a general exclamation of surprise, and the governor of the feast, crying out, 'A great prophet indeed hath been among us, and we knew it not!' rose to approach and do honor to Jesus; but he had already conveyed himself away, at once rising and passing out through the door, and seeking the solitude of the gardens."

The rumor of the miracle at Cana has reached Jerusalem since I began this letter, and I hear that it has produced no little excitement in the market-places and courts of the Temple. Rabbi Amos, on his return from sacrifice, a few minutes ago, said that he saw, in the court of the Temple, more than thirty priests with rolls of the Prophets in their hands, engaged in looking up the prophecies of the Christ.

Your affectionate daughter,

Adina.

LETTER XIV.

My Dear Father:

You will not require the testimony of my letters to enable you to appreciate the fame of the wonderful young man of Nazareth, Jesus, of whose works you must have heard ere this. His fame for wisdom, for knowledge of the Scriptures, for power to teach, and for miracles, has gone abroad through all Syria, so that they bring to him sick persons, both rich and poor, even from Damascus, to be healed of him; and he heals all who are brought unto him, whether possessed of devils, lunatic, or having the palsy. While I now write, a company is passing the open window, bearing upon beds two wealthy men of Jerusalem, given over by their physicians, who are going to him to be cured.

"So great is the multitude which everywhere follows Jesus," writes John to Mary, "that he is often compelled to withdraw from them by stealth, to get to some by-place of quiet where he can refresh his wearied strength for a few days. At such times we, who are his immediate followers, have the benefit of his teaching and private instructions. But he cannot remain long away from the people. They soon penetrate his retirement. How wonderful is he who thus holds in his hands divine power! The authority of kings is nothing before that which he possesses in his voice; yet he is serene, humble, oh, how humble! to our shame; and always calm and gentle. He spends much time in private prayer to God, whom he always addresses as his Father. Never was such a man on earth. We, who know him most intimately, stand most in awe of him; yet with our deep reverence for his holy character is combined the purest affection. In one and the same breath I feel that I adore him as my Lord, and love him even as my brother. So we all feel toward him."

Such, my dear father, is the tenor of all John's letters. When we shall see Jesus at Jerusalem, I shall be able from personal observation to write to you more particularly concerning his doctrines and miracles. What is also of importance, it has been proven by the results of the examination made by some of the scribes of the Temple, that he was truly born in Bethlehem, and that both his mother Mary, and Joseph her husband, are lineal descendants of the house of David. Moreover Phineas, the venerable priest, whom you know, hath borne testimony to the fact that when Jesus was an infant, during the reign of the elder Herod, there arrived in Jerusalem three eminent princes, men of wisdom and learning. One of these came from Persia, one from the Grecian province of Media, and one from Arabia, and brought with them gifts of gold and spices, and were attended by retinues. These three princes reached Jerusalem the same day by three different ways, and entered by three different gates, each unknowing to the other's presence or object, till they met in the city before Herod's palace. One represented himself descended from Shem, another from Japhet, the third from Ham. And they mysteriously, it is said, typified all the races of the earth who by them recognized and adored the Savior of men in the child Jesus. The king, hearing that these three strangers had arrived in Jerusalem, sent to know wherefore they had honored his kingdom with a visit. "They answered," says Phineas, "that they came to do homage to the young prince, who was born king of the Jews." And when Herod asked what prince they spoke of, they answered, "We have seen his star in the East, and are come to worship him."

"Hereupon," says Phineas, "the king issued an edict for all the chief priests and scribes of the people to assemble in the council chamber of his palace. He then addressed them:

"'Ye to whom is given the care of the books of the Law and the Prophets, whose study they are, and in whom lies the skill to interpret the prophecies, search therein, and tell me truly where the Christ is to be born. Behold here present these august and wise men who have come from afar to do him homage; nay more, as they aver, to worship him as God. Let us have the courtesy to give them the answer that they seek, and let us not be found more ignorant of these things than those who dwell in other lands.'

"Several of the chief priests then rose and said: 'It is known, O king, to all who are Jews, and who read the Prophets, that Messias cometh of the house of David, of the town of Bethlehem; for thus it is written by the prophet: "And thou, Bethlehem, in the land of Judah, art not least among the princes of Judah, for out of thee shall come a governor that shall rule my people Israel."'

"This question being thus decided," continued Phineas, "Herod dismissed the council, and retiring to his own private room, secretly sent to the three princes of the East to inquire of them what time the star appeared. He then said to them:

"'You have my permission, noble strangers, to go to Bethlehem, and search for the young child: and when ye have found him, bring me word again, that I may come and worship him also.' Then they left the presence of Herod, and it being dark when they left the palace, they were overjoyed to behold the star which they saw in the East, going before them. They followed it until it left Jerusalem by the Bethlehem gate, and it led them on to the town of Bethlehem, and stopped above an humble dwelling therein. When they were come into the house, they saw the rays of the star resting upon the head of an infant in the arms of its mother Mary, the wife of Joseph. They at once acknowledged and hailed him as Prince and King of Israel, and falling down, worshiped him; and opening their treasures, they presented unto him gold, frankincense and myrrh, gifts that are offered on the altar to God alone."

When Phineas was asked by Caiaphas how he knew this fact, he answered that he himself, prompted by curiosity to see the prince they had come to worship, had followed them out of the palace of Herod, out of the gate, and even into Bethlehem, and witnessed their prostrations and offerings to the infant child of Mary. "And," he added, "if this be doubted, there are many Jews now living in Jerusalem, and a certain Hebrew captain, now stricken in years, who can testify to the slaughter, by Herod's command, of the infants of Bethlehem; for this captain, Jeremias, led on the soldiers."

"And wherefore this slaughter?" asked Caiaphas. "It is not on record."

"Kings do not record their deeds of violence," answered Phineas. "Herod kept it hushed up when he found that he gained nothing by it but hatred. He slew them in order that the infant Jesus might be destroyed among them; for the three wise men, instead of returning through Jerusalem to their own country, and informing him where they had found the child, departed by another way. But the child escaped, doubtless by God's powerful protection."

"Dost thou believe in him also?" asked Caiaphas, with angry surprise, looking sternly on Phineas.

"I will first see and hear him speak, and if he be proven to me to be Messias, I will gladly worship him."

"Hereupon," said Rabbi Amos, "there arose a great uproar, some crying that Jesus was the Christ, and others that Phineas should be stoned to death."

Thus you see, my dear father, how the evidence increases in value and importance, proving Jesus to be the Messiah. Tell me, is not this the Christ?

Your affectionate and loving,

Adina.

LETTER XV.

My Dear Father:

The inquiry you made in your last letter, "What hath become of the prophet of Jordan, since the fame of Jesus hath so eclipsed his own?" I can answer but with sadness. The mission on which John came terminated when Jesus came. Soon afterwards he left the wilderness and entered Jericho, where Herod chanced to be visiting. Here he preached in the public places, and in the market, and on the very steps of the Governor's palace. Now while he was thus speaking to the people, and the officers and soldiers of the Tetrarch's guard, Herod himself came forth upon the balcony to listen. The prophet no sooner beheld him than he boldly addressed him, and sternly reproved him for the sin of having married the wife of his brother Philip, contrary to the law. Now Herod, it is said, did not show resentment at his plain dealings, but, inviting the prophet into his hall, talked much with him, and in parting offered him gifts, which John refused to touch. The next day he sent for him again to ask him some questions touching the Messias of whom he preached. Now Herodia, when it was reported to her, after the return of Herod from Jericho to his Tetrarchy, how that the prophet had publicly spoken against her marriage with Herod, became very angry; and when she found that John was still favored by her husband, she sent for Herod and said that if he would please her he must throw the prophet of Jordan into prison. At length Herod yielded, against his own will, and gave orders for the arrest of the prophet; who, the same night, was thrown into the ward of the castle. For some weeks this holy man, whose only offense was that he had the courage to reprove sin in high places, remained in bonds, while Herod each day sought to find some excuse for releasing him without displeasing Herodia, of whose anger he stood in great fear, being an abject slave to his love for her. At length the birthday of Herod arrived, and he conveyed word to John that in honor of the day he would send and fetch him out of prison as soon as he should obtain the consent of his wife, which he believed she would accord to him on such an anniversary.

Now, after the feast, Philippa, the daughter of Herodia, and of her former husband Philip, came in and danced before Prince Herod; and being beautiful in person and full of grace in every motion, she so pleased her step-father that he made a great oath, having drunk much wine with his guests, that he would give her whatsoever she would ask, were it the half of his kingdom. Her mother then called her, and whispered to her imperatively.

"Give me," said the maiden, turning towards Herod, "the head, now, of John the Baptist in a charger."

The Tetrarch no sooner heard this request than he turned pale, and said fiercely:

"Thy mother hath been tampering with thine ears, girl. Ask half of my kingdom and I will give it thee, but let me not shed blood on my birthday."

"Wilt thou falsify thine oath?" asked his wife, scornfully.

"For mine oath's sake, and for those who have heard it, I will grant thy desire," he at length answered, with a sigh of regret and self-reproach. He then turned to the captain of the guard and commanded him to slay John Baptist in prison, and bring presently there his head upon a charger.

At the end of a quarter of an hour, which was passed by Herod in great excitement, walking up and down the floor, and by his guests in silent expectation, the door opened, and the captain of the guard entered, followed by the executioner, who carried a brazen platter upon which lay the gory head of the eloquent forerunner of Christ.

"Give it to her!" cried Herod, sternly, waving him towards the beautiful maiden who stood near the inner door. The executioner placed the charger in her hands; and, with a smile of triumph, she bore it to her mother, who had retired to an inner room.

All the disciples of the murdered prophet then went where Jesus was preaching and healing, and told him what had been done to John. "When Jesus heard of the death of John, he was very sorrowful," writes John to Mary, "and went away into a desert place apart." In the meanwhile the disciples of John Baptist fled, some into the deserts, while others sought Jesus to protect and counsel them. At length he found himself surrounded by a great multitude, chiefly of John's disciples, besides many who had come to hear him preach and be healed of him. The place was a desert and far from any town. Forgetful of all else, save following Jesus, they were without food. "Which," says John, writing to Rabbi Amos, "we who were his disciples seeing, suggested that Jesus should send them away to the villages to buy themselves victuals. But Jesus answered us, and said quietly:

"'They need not go away; give ye them to eat.'

"And Simon said, 'Master, where can we get bread for so many? We have among us but five loaves and two small fishes.'

"Upon hearing this, Jesus said, 'It is enough; bring them hither to me.'

"We collected the bread and fishes, and I, myself, laid them upon a rock before Jesus. He then said to us, 'Command the multitude to sit down on the grass.' And when they were all seated, he took the five loaves and laying his hands upon them and upon the two fishes, he looked up to heaven and blessed them, and then, breaking them into fragments, he gave them to us his disciples, and bade us distribute to the people. As often as we would return for more, we found the loaves and the fishes undiminished, and I saw with wonder how, when this Prophet of God would break off a piece of one of the fishes or of a loaf, the same part would immediately be seen thereon as if it had not been separated; and in this manner he continued to break and distribute to us for nearly an hour, until all ate as much as they would. When no one demanded more, he commanded us to gather up the fragments which lay by his side, and there were twelve baskets full over and above what was needed. The number that was thus miraculously fed was about five thousand men, besides nearly an equal number of women and children. And this mighty Prophet, who could thus feed an army, voluntarily suffered forty days and nights the pangs of hunger in the desert! He seems a man in suffering, a God in creating!"

This wonderful miracle, my dear father, is one that has too many witnesses to be denied. Not a day passes that we do not hear of some still more extraordinary exhibition of his power than the preceding. Every morning, when men meet in the market places, or in the corridors of the Temple, the first inquiry is, "What new wonder has he performed? Have you heard of another miracle of this mighty Prophet?" The priests alone are offended, and speak evil of him through envy.

They even have gone so far as to assert that he performs his miracles by magic, or by the aid of Beelzebub, the prince of the devils. "If we suffer him to take men's minds as he doth," said Caiaphas to Rabbi Amos yesterday, when he heard that Jesus had walked on the sea to join his disciples in their ship, and stilled a tempest with a word, "the worship in the Temple will be at an end, and the sacrifice will cease. He draweth all men unto him."

You have asked, dear father, in your letter, "Where is Elias, who is to precede Messias, according to the prophet Malachi?" This question Jesus himself has answered, says John, when a rabbi put it to him. He replied thus:

"Elias has come already, and ye have done unto him whatsoever ye listed."

"Dost thou speak of John the Baptist?" asked those about him, when they heard this.

"John came in the spirit and power of Elias, and therefore was he thus called by the prophet," was the answer of Jesus.

I did not tell you that besides the six disciples whom I have named, he has chosen six others, which twelve he keeps near his person as his more favored followers, and whom he daily instructs in the doctrines he came down from heaven to teach. Of the thousands who never weary of going from place to place in his train, he has also selected seventy men, whom he has despatched by twos into every city and village of Judea, commanding them to proclaim the kingdom of God is at hand, and that the time when men everywhere should repent and turn to God, has come.

It is now commonly reported that he will be here at the Passover. I shall then behold him, and, like the wise men, I shall worship him with mingled awe and love. I will again write you, dear father, after I see and hear him. Till then, believe me your affectionate daughter,

Adina.

LETTER XVI.

My Dear Father:

While I write, the city is agitated like a tumultuous sea. The loud murmurs of the multitudes in the streets, and even in the distant market-place, reach my startled ears. A squadron of Roman cavalry has just thundered past towards the Temple, where the uproar is greatest; for a rumor of an insurrection begun among the people has come to Pilate the Procurator.

I will relate to you the circumstance in detail.

Yesterday Mary's cousin, John, returned and came unexpectedly into the hall of the fountain, in the rear of the house, where we were all seated in the cool of the vines. Uncle Amos was in the act of reading to us from the Prophet Jeremiah, a prophecy relating to the Messias that is to come (nay, that is come, dear father), when John appeared. Mary's blushes welcomed him and showed how dear he was to her. Uncle Amos embraced and kissed him and seated him by us, and called for a servant to bathe his feet, for he was dusty and travel-worn. From him we learned that his beloved Master, Jesus, had reached Bethany, and was reposing from his fatigues at the hospitable though humble house of Lazarus, Mary and Martha. When we heard this, we were all very glad; and Uncle Amos particularly seemed to experience the deepest satisfaction.

"If he come into Jerusalem," said he warmly, "he shall be my guest. Bid him to my roof, O John, that my household may be blessed in having a prophet of God step across its threshold."

"I will tell my beloved Master thy wish, Rabbi Amos," answered John. "Doubtless, as he has no home nor friends in the city, he will remain under your roof."

"Say not no friends!" I exclaimed. "We are all his friends here, and fain would be his disciples."

"What! Rabbi Amos also?" cried John, with a glance of pleasure and surprise at the venerable priest of God.

"Yes, I am ready, after all that I have seen and heard, I am ready to confess him a prophet sent from God."

"He is far more than a prophet, O Rabbi Amos," answered John. "Never prophet did the works Jesus does. It seems that all power is at his command. If you witnessed what I witness daily, as he traverses Judea, you would say that he was Jehovah descended to earth in human form."

"Nay, do not blaspheme, young man," said Rabbi Amos, with some severity of reproof.

John bowed his head in reverence to the rebuke of the Rabbi, but nevertheless answered respectfully and firmly. "Never man did like him. If he be not God in the flesh, he is an angel in flesh invested with divine power."

"If he be the Messiah," I said, "he cannot be an angel, for are not the prophecies clear that the Messiah shall be 'a man of sorrows'? Is he not to be 'the seed of the woman'? a man and not an angel?"

"Yes," answered John, "you remember well the prophecies. I firmly believe Jesus to be the Messiah, the Son of God. Yet, what he is more than man, what he is less than God, is incomprehensible to me and to my fellow-disciples. We wonder, love and adore! At one moment we feel like embracing him as a brother dearly beloved; at another, we are ready to fall at his feet and worship him. I have seen him weep at beholding the miseries of the diseased wretches which were dragged into his presence, and then with a touch—with a word, heal them; and they would stand before him in the purity and beauty of health and strong manhood."

"And yet," said Nicodemus, a rich Pharisee, who entered as John was first speaking, and listened without interrupting, "and yet, young man, I heard you say that Jesus, of whom you and all men relate such mighty deeds, has remained at Bethany to recover from his fatigue. How can a man who holds all sickness in his power, be subject to mere weariness of body? I would say unto him, Physician, heal thyself!"

This was spoken with a tone of incredulity by this learned ruler of the Jews, and, stroking his snowy beard, he waited of John a reply.

"So far as I can learn the character of Jesus," replied John, "his healing power over diseases is not for his own good. He uses his power to work miracles for the benefit of others through love and compassion. Being a man with this divine power dwelling in him for us, he is subject to infirmities as a man; he hungers, thirsts, wearies, suffers, as a man. I have seen him heal a nobleman's son by a word, and the next moment seat himself, supporting his aching head upon his hand, looking pale and languid, for his labors of love are vast, and he is often overcome by them. Once Simon Peter, seeing him ready to sink with weariness, after healing all day, asked him and said, 'Master, thou givest strength to others; why suffer thyself, when all health and strength are in thee as in a living well, to be weary?'

"'It is not my desire to escape human infirmities by any power my Father hath bestowed upon me for the good of men. Through suffering only can I draw all men after me!' he replied."

John said this so sadly, as if he were repeating the very tones in which Jesus had spoken it, that we all remained silent for a few moments. I felt tears fill my eyes, and I was glad to see that the proud Pharisee, Nicodemus, looked moved. After a full minute's serious pause, he said:

"This man is doubtless no common prophet. When he comes into the city, I shall be glad to hear from his own mouth his doctrines, and to witness some potent miracle."

"Prophet he is, without doubt," answered Amos. "It is not the question now whether he be a prophet or not; for the hundreds he has healed are living witnesses that he has the spirit and power of the old prophets, and is truly a prophet. The question that remains is, whether he be the Messiah or not."

Nicodemus slowly and negatively shook his head, and then answered:

"Messias cometh not out of Galilee."

At this moment a sudden wild, joyful cry from Mary thrilled our nerves, and looking towards the door, we saw her folded in the arms of a young man whom I had never seen before. My surprise had not time to form itself into any definite explanation of what I saw, when I beheld the young man, who was exceedingly handsome and the picture of health, after kissing the clinging Mary upon her cheeks, leave her to throw himself into the arms of Rabbi Amos, crying:

"My father, my dear father!"

My uncle, who had stood amazed and wonderingly gazing on him, as if he could not believe what his eyes beheld, now burst into profound expressions of grateful joy, and as he clasped the young stranger to his heart, fell upon his neck and wept, with scarcely power to articulate the words:

"My son! My son! Lost, but found again! This is the Lord's doing and is marvelous in our eyes!"

John also embraced the new-comer, and the ruler stood silent with wonder. While I was looking bewildered upon the scene, Mary ran and said to me, with tears of gladness shining in her dark, fine eyes:

"It is Benjamin, my lost brother, beloved Adina!"

"I did not know you had a brother," I answered in surprise.

"We have long regarded him as dead," she replied with mingled emotions. "Seven years ago he became lunatic, and fled to the tombs without the city, where he has long dwelt with many others who were possessed with devils. For years he has neither spoken to nor known us. But oh, now—now behold him! It seems a vision! See how manly, noble, like himself he is, with the same intelligent, smiling eyes."

She then flew to take him by the hand and lead him toward me, all eyes being fixed upon him, as if he had been a spirit.

When he saw their wondering gaze, he said:

"It is I, both son and brother to those dearest to me. I am in my right mind and well."

"Who has effected this change, so extraordinary, oh, my son?" inquired Rabbi Amos, with trembling lips, and keeping his hand on Benjamin's shoulder, as if he feared he would vanish away.

"It was Jesus, the Prophet of the Highest!" answered he, with solemn gratitude.

"Jesus!" we all exclaimed in one voice.

"I could have said so," answered John, calmly. "Rabbi Nicodemus, thou knowest this young man well. Thou hast known him in childhood, and beheld him in the madness of his lunacy among the tombs. Dost thou doubt now whether Jesus be the very Christ?"

Nicodemus made no reply, but I saw from the expression of his face that he believed.

"How was this done to thee, young man?" he asked, with deep and visible emotion.

"I was wandering near Bethany this morning," answered the restored one, with modesty, "when I beheld a crowd which I madly followed. As I drew near I beheld in their midst a man, whom I had no sooner cast my eyes upon than I felt seize me an ungovernable propensity to destroy him. The same fury possessed seven others, my comrades in madness, and together we rushed upon him, with great stones and knives in our hands. The crowd gave way and fell back aghast, and called him to save himself. But he moved not, but, left alone in a wide space, stood calmly awaiting us. We were within a few feet of him, and I was nearest, ready to strike him to the earth, when he quietly lifted one finger and said, 'Peace!' We stood immovable, without power to stir a foot, while our rage and hatred increased with our inability to harm him. We howled and foamed at the mouth before him, for we then knew that he was the Son of God, come to destroy us.

"'Come out of the men and depart quickly!' he said, in a tone of command as if to us, but really to the demons within us. At this word I fell at his feet in a dreadful convulsion, and my whole body writhed as if it had been wrestling with an invisible demon. Jesus then stooped and laid his hand upon my brow and said, 'Son, arise. Thou art made whole!'

"At these words a black cloud seemed to be lifted from my mind. The glory of a new existence appeared to dawn upon my soul, while his voice melted my heart within me. Bursting into tears, the first I have shed for seven years, I fell at his feet and kissed and embraced them."

When Benjamin had done speaking, we all gave glory to God, who had given him back to us, and who had sent so great a Prophet among men.

I commenced this letter, dearest father, by an allusion to a great commotion which is agitating the whole city, but as I have taken up so much of this letter in relating what passed yesterday in the hall of the fountain, I will leave the account of the tumult for my next letter, which I shall write this evening.

May the God of our fathers be with you, and bless you and the holy people of the promise.

Adina.

LETTER XVII.

My Dear Father:

When, on the morning of the Passover, it was noised abroad that the Prophet of Galilee was entering the city by the gate of Jericho, the whole city was stirred, and from houses and shops poured forth crowds which turned their steps in that direction. Mary and I went upon the house-top, hoping to see something; but far and near was visible only a sea of heads, from which a deep murmuring arose, like the ceaseless voice of the ocean chafing upon a rocky shore. The top of the gate-way was visible from the place where we stood, but it was black with the people who had crowded upon it to look down. There was heard at length an immense shout, as of one voice, which was followed by a swaying and onward pressure of the crowds.

"The Prophet must have entered the gate," said my Cousin Mary, breathlessly. "How they do him honor! It is the reception of a king!"

We were in hopes he would pass by our house, as we were on one of the chief thoroughfares, but were disappointed, as he ascended the hill of Moriah to the Temple. A part of the ascent to the house of the Lord is visible from our roof, and we had the satisfaction of seeing the Prophet at a distance. We knew him only because he was in advance. The nighest one to him, Mary said, was her Cousin John, though at that distance I could not have recognized him. The head of the multitude disappeared beneath the arch of the Temple, and thousands upon thousands followed after; and in the rear rode the young Roman centurion, whom I have before spoken of, at the head of four hundred horse, to keep order in the vast mass. Mary could not recognize him, saying it was too far to tell who he was; but I knew him, not only by his air and bearing, but by the scarlet pennon that fluttered from his iron lance, and which I had bestowed upon him, for he told me he had lost one his fair Roman sister, Tullia, had given him, and as he so much regretted its loss, I supplied its place by another, worked by my own hands.

STREET IN JERUSALEM

The multitude, as many as could gain admission, having entered the great gate of the Temple, for a few minutes there was a profound stillness. Mary said:

"He is worshiping or sacrificing now."

"Perhaps," I said, "he is addressing the people, and they listen to his words."

While I was speaking there arose from the bosom of the Temple a loud, irregular, strange outcry of a thousand voices, pitched to high excitement. The people without the gate responded by a universal shout, and then we beheld those nighest the walls retreat down the hillside in terrified confusion, while, to increase the tumult, the Roman horse charged up the hill, seeking to penetrate the masses to reach the gate out of which the people poured like a living and tempest-tossed river, before which the head of the cohort recoiled or was overwhelmed and down-trodden! I held my breath in dreadful suspense, not knowing the cause of the fearful scene we beheld, nor to what it might lead. Mary sank, almost insensible, by my side. A quarter of an hour had not passed when young Samuel Ben Azel, who had the day before come up from Nain to the Passover with his mother, entered and explained to us the cause of the scene I had witnessed.

"The Prophet Jesus, having entered into the Temple, found all the courts filled with merchants, changers of money, and sellers of cattle to the sacrificers. Portions of the sacred place were divided off by fences, in which hundreds of sheep and cattle were stalled. On his way to the inner Temple the Prophet found his path so obstructed by the stalls and the tables of the brokers, that he had to go around them, and often to turn back and take a less hedged-up avenue. At length finding, upon the very lintel of the Court of the Priests, a priest himself engaged at a table as a money-changer, and near him a Levite keeping a stall for selling doves and sparrows to the worshipers, he stopped upon the step, and turning round, cast his eye, which now beamed with an awful majesty and power, over the scene of noisy commerce and bartering. Every face was turned towards him in expectation. The half-completed bargain was suspended, and buyer and seller directed their gaze, as by a sort of fascination, not unmingled with a strange fear and awe, upon him. Those who had crowded about him drew back farther and farther, slowly but irresistibly widening the space between them and him, they knew not by what impulse, till he stood alone, save near him remained John, his disciple. The uproar of the buying and selling suddenly subsided, and the loud lowing of the cattle and the bleating of the sheep stopped as if a supernatural awe had seized even the brute creation at his presence, and only the soft cooing of doves stirred the vast, death-like stillness of the place, a moment before a scene of oaths, cries, shouts, of running to and fro, buying and selling, the ringing of money, and the buzz of ten thousand voices! It was as if a hurricane, sweeping with deafening uproar of the elements over the lashed ocean, had been suddenly arrested and followed by a great calm. The silence was dreadful! It stopped the very beating of my heart. Every eye of the vast multitude seemed to fasten itself on the Prophet in expectation of some dread event. The step of the Temple upon which he stood seemed to be a throne, and the people before him expecting judgment. Suddenly the silence was broken by a young man near me who gave a piercing shriek, and fell insensible upon the marble floor. There was a general thrill of horror, yet the same awful stillness succeeded this startling interruption. That one intense shriek had spoken for us all. Suddenly the voice of the Prophet was heard, clear, authoritative, and ringing like the trumpet that shook Sinai when the Law was given.

"'It is written, My Father's house shall be called a house of prayer; but ye have made it a den of thieves!'

"He then picked up from the pavement at his feet a small cord, which some one had thrown down, and doubling it in the form of a scourge, he advanced. Before his presence fled the changers of money, priests and Levites, sellers of oxen, sellers of sheep, sellers of doves, leaving their property to its fate.

"'Take these things hence,' cried the Prophet; 'make not my Father's house a house of merchandise!'

"Such a scene of confusion and flight was never witnessed as now followed! In the moment of panic I was borne along with the current. Money tables were overturned on all sides, but not the most avaricious one present thought, at that moment, of stopping to gather any of the gold and silver which the rushing thousands trampled beneath their feet. It was not the whip of small cords before which we fled, for he touched no man therewith, but it was from the majesty of his countenance. To the eyes of all the little whip seemed to blaze and flash above their heads, as if it were the fiery sword of a destroying angel. In a few moments the Priests' Court of the Temple was cleared of every soul, as we fled towards the South gate. On looking back, I saw that the Prophet pursued not, but stood alone, Master and Lord of the Temple. The whip was no longer in his hand, and his whole attitude and expression of face seemed changed from their late impress to an air of the profoundest compassion, as he looked after us, still flying from his presence."

My uncle, Rabbi Amos, who, on his return from the Temple, corroborated what Samuel had stated, added that as Jesus stood alone, possessor of the gold-strewn floors of the courts of the Temple, the High Priest advanced towards him, and with awe, not unmixed with anger, demanded of him by what authority he did these things.

His answer was, "My Father's house must not be made a house of merchandise."

"Art thou the Christ?" asked the High Priest, still standing some distance off from him.

"If I tell thee that I am, ye will not believe."

"What sign showest thou that thou art sent, and hast authority to do what thou doest here to-day within the Temple?"

"Hast thou not had proof of my power from heaven?" answered Jesus, stretching forth his hand towards the still terror-stricken multitude; and then laying it upon his breast, he added: "Destroy this temple, and in three days I will raise it up! Be this to you, O priest, and to all Judea, the sign that I am sent by my Father who is in heaven. As he hath given me commandment, so I do!"

At this there was a great murmuring, said Rabbi Amos, for many of the priests, with Annas also, had got boldness and drawn near to hear.

"He cannot be a just man," said Annas, "nor doth he honor God, if he would have us destroy the Temple."

"Yet if he be not sent of God, whence hath he this power over men?" answered another.

"He doeth this by Beelzebub, whose prophet he doubtless is," said Annas, in a loud tone, "for a true prophet would not seek the destruction of God's holy house."

Thereupon there was a multitude of voices, some crying one thing, and some another. Caiaphas at length obtained silence, and said to him with awe:

"Art thou that Christ of the Prophets?"

"I am!" calmly and firmly answered the Prophet; and, raising his eyes to heaven, he added impressively, "I am come down from God."

When, adds my uncle, Annas heard this, he lifted up his voice in an exclamation of horror, and cried out:

"Hear ye this blasphemer! Let us cast him forth from the Temple which he pollutes!"

But no man dared approach the Prophet.

"Bear witness," then said he, sorrowfully, rather than in anger, "that I have come unto my own, and ye have received me not! This Temple of my Father, from which you would drive me forth, shall no longer be the dwelling place and altar of Jehovah. The day cometh when your priesthood shall be taken away and given to others, and among the Gentiles shall arise my Father's name, on every hill and in every valley of the earth, holy temples, wherein he shall delight to dwell; and men shall no longer need to worship God in Zion, but in all places shall prayer and praise be offered to the Most High. This Temple, which ye have polluted, shall be overthrown, and ye shall be scattered among the nations."

Thus speaking, the Prophet quitted the Temple, leaving the High Priest and priests and Levites standing gazing after him, without power to utter a word.

Such, my dear father, is the account given by Rabbi Amos of what passed in the Temple. That Jesus is the Christ is now beyond question, for he has openly acknowledged it to the High Priest.

Adieu, dearest father. The servants are bringing in boughs for the booths, and I must close this letter, with prayers to our fathers' God for your peace and welfare.

Adina.

LETTER XVIII.

My Dear Father:

You say in your letter, which I received from the hands of the Roman courier, that you have read with interest all my letters, and more especially those which relate to Jesus of Galilee. You say that you are ready to acknowledge him as a prophet sent from God. But you add, "He can have no claim to be the Christ, because he comes out of Galilee."

To this objection, dear father, Rabbi Amos desires me to say that he has investigated the records of births kept in the Temple, and finds, as I have before named to you, that Jesus was born in Bethlehem. He afterwards removed with his parents to Egypt, and thence returning to Judea, settled in Galilee, where he was brought up. Of these facts in his history not only Rabbi Amos is satisfied, but Nicodemus also, whose learning you will not gainsay; and the latter, very much to our surprise, and my own delight, added yesterday, when we were talking over the subject at supper, "There is a prophecy, O Rabbi Amos, which strengthens this mighty Prophet's claim to be the Messias."

"What is it? Let me hear all that can strengthen!" I asked earnestly; not, dear father, that my confidence in him needs confirmation, but I wish others to believe.

"You will find it in the Prophet Hoseas," answered Nicodemus, "and thus it readeth: 'I have called my son out of Egypt.'"

My heart bounded with joy, dear father, at hearing this prophecy named; but judge my emotion when Nicodemus, taking the roll of the Prophet Isaiah in his hand, read the words that follow, and applied them to Jesus: "Beyond Jordan, in Galilee of the Gentiles, the people which sat in darkness have seen a great light!" This changes the objection to his coming from Galilee into additional proof of his claim to be the Messias.

In my last letter I informed you that Rabbi Amos had invited him to sojourn with us during the Passover. He graciously accepted the invitation, and came hither yesterday, after he had quitted the Temple, from which he had with such commanding power driven forth the merchants and money-changers.

Hearing, while expecting him, the rumor flying along the streets, "The Prophet comes! The Prophet comes!" uttered by hundreds of voices of men and children, I hastened to the house-top. The whole way was a sea of heads. The multitude came rolling onward, like a mighty river; as I have seen the dark Nile flow when pouring its freshening floods along its confined banks.

Mary stood by my side. We tried to single out the central person around whom undulated the sea of heads; but all was so wildly confused with the waving of palm branches that we could distinguish nothing clearly. While I was straining my gaze to make out the form of the Prophet, Mary touched me, and bade me look in the opposite direction. As I did so I beheld Æmilius Tullius, the young Roman centurion, now Prefect of Pilate's Legion, advancing at the head of two hundred horsemen at full spur, in order to meet and turn back the advancing column of people.

As he came opposite the house he looked up, and seeing us upon the parapet, he gracefully waved his gleaming sword, saluted us, and was dashing past, when Mary cried out:

"Noble sir, there is no insurrection, as some of the people have doubtless told thee, but this vast crowd moving hitherwards is only an escort to the Prophet of Nazareth, who cometh to be my father's guest."

"I have orders from Pilate to arrest him, lady, as a disturber of the peace of the capital."

"Shall a prophet suffer because his mighty deeds draw crowds after his footsteps, noble Roman? If thy troops advance there will be a collision with the people. If thou wilt withdraw them a little, thou wilt see that when the Prophet crosses my father's threshold, they will go away in peace."

The prefect said nothing, but seemed to look at me for some words; which seeing, I earnestly entreated him to do the Prophet no violence.

"For thy wishes' sake, lady, I will here halt my troop, especially as I see that the people are unarmed."

The centurion then gave orders to his horsemen to draw up in line opposite the house. The multitude now came near, but many of those in advance, seeing the Roman horse, stopped or fell into the rear, so that I beheld Jesus appear in front, walking at an even, calm pace, John at his side; also Rabbi Amos was with him. As he came nigher, the people, for fear of the long Roman spears, kept back, and he advanced almost alone. I saw John point out to him our house. The Prophet raised his face and gazed upon it an instant. I saw his features full. His countenance was not that of a young man, but of a person past the middle age of life, though he is but thirty. His hair was mingled with gray, and in his finely shaped, oval face were carved, evidently by care and sorrow, deep lines. His flowing beard fell upon his breast. His eyes appeared to be fixed upon us both for an instant with benignity and peace. Deep sadness, gentle, not stern, seemed to be the characteristic expression of his noble and princely visage. There was an air of manly dignity in his carriage and mien, and as he walked amid his followers he was truly kingly, yet simplicity and humility qualified this native majesty of port. He seemed to draw out both the awe and love of those who saw him—to command equally our homage and sympathy.

Passing the troop of horse, John and Rabbi Amos conducted Jesus to our door; but before they reached it there was a loud cry from several harsh voices to the Roman to arrest him. On looking from whence these shouts came, I saw that they proceeded from several of the priests, headed by Annas, who were pressing forward through the crowd, crying menacingly:

"We call upon you, O prefect, to arrest this man! Shame on thee, Rabbi Amos! Hast thou also believed in the impostor? We charge this Galilean, O Roman, with having made sedition. He has taken possession of the Temple, and unless you see to it he will have the citadel out of your hands. If you arrest him not, we will not answer for the consequences that may befall the city and the people."

"I see nothing to fear from this man, O ye Jews," answered Æmilius. "He is unarmed and without troops. Stand back; keep ye to your Temple! It is from your outcries comes all the confusion! Back to your altars! If commotions arise in the city, Pilate will make you accountable. All the rest of the people are peaceable save yourselves."

"We will take our complaint before the Procurator!" cried Annas, who was the chief speaker; and, followed by a large company of angry priests and Levites, with staves in their hands, he took his way towards the palace of the Roman Governor.

I looked my gratitude to Æmilius for so fearlessly taking part with the Prophet.

The multitude now began to retire as the Roman horse slowly moved up the street. Jesus was received into the house by Mary, and taken into the inner hall, where, water being brought, Rabbi Amos himself removed the sandals of the Prophet and reverently washed his feet, while Mary, to do him all honor, dried them with a rich veil, which she had just worked in anticipation of her coming bridal with her Cousin John. It was at this moment I entered the hall.

There were in the room not only Amos, and John, and Mary, but the Priest Elias, cousin to Caiaphas, who, desirous of hearing from the lips of the Prophet his sublime teachings, had come in with him. There were also present five men whom I never saw before, but who, John said, were his disciples. I, however, had no eye or ear for any one but Jesus. I saw that he seemed very weary and pale, and for the first time I noticed he seemed to suffer, as from time to time he raised his hand to his temples. Desirous of serving so holy a person, I hastened to prepare a restorative which, bringing it into the hall, I was about to give to him, when the Priest Elias put me rudely back and said, "Nay, maiden, let us witness a miracle!" He then turned to the Prophet and said, "Master, we have heard much of thy power to do miracles, but have seen none by thee. If thou wilt presently show me a miracle, I will believe, I and all my house. Thou hast a pain in thy forehead; heal it with a touch, and I will acknowledge thee the Christ, the Son of the Blessed!"

Jesus turned his eyes upon him and said, "Elias, thou readest the Prophets, and shouldest know whether he who speaketh unto thee be the Christ or no. Search the Scriptures, that thou mayest know that the time of his visitation is come, and that I am he. I do no miracles to relieve my own suffering. I came into this world to suffer. Isaiah wrote of me as a man of sorrows, and acquainted with grief. Blessed are they who, not seeing, shall believe!"

"But, Master," said the aged Levite, Asher, "we know whence thou art— even from Galilee. But when Christ cometh, no man knoweth whence he is."

"It is true, O man of Israel, ye both know me and whence I am. Yet ye know not him who sent me. Ye do not understand the Scriptures or ye would indeed know me, whence I am, and who hath sent me. But ye know neither me nor him that sent me, for I am come out from God. If ye had known him, ye would know me also. The time cometh when ye shall know whence I am and believe in me; but now your hearts are darkened through ignorance and unbelieving."

When he had thus spoken with great dignity and power, there were many present who were offended, and some voices murmured against him. Then Rabbi Amos led him forth to the apartment he had prepared for him.

In going to it the Prophet had to cross the court, and as I was watching his retiring footsteps, I saw four men, who had climbed to the house-top from the side street, the doors being closed, let down a fifth in a blanket at the very feet of Jesus. It was a man afflicted with the palsy, and their own father. Jesus, seeing their filial love, stopped and said kindly:

"Young men, what would ye have me to do?"

"Heal our aged father, holy Rabbi."

"Believe ye that I can do this?" he asked, fixing his gaze earnestly on them.

"Yes, Lord, we believe that thou art the Christ, the Son of the living God! All things are possible unto thee!"

Jesus looked benignantly upon them, and then taking the venerable man by the hand, he said to him in a loud voice, so that all who were looking on heard him:

"Aged father, I say unto thee, arise and walk!"

The palsied man instantly rose to his feet, whole and strong, and after casting a glance around upon himself, he threw himself at the Prophet's feet and bathed them in tears. The four sons followed their father's example, while all the people who witnessed the miracle shouted, "Glory to God, who hath given such power unto men!"

Such, my dear father, are the increasing testimonies Jesus bears, by miracles as well as by words, to his being Messias.

The God of our fathers keep you in health.

Your loving daughter,

Adina.

LETTER XIX.

My Dear Father:

The visit of the Prophet Jesus to the city has produced results of the most amazing character. The priesthood is divided. Caiaphas has publicly recognized him as a prophet, while Annas has publicly declared that he is an impostor; and thus two parties are formed in the city, headed by the two priests, and most men have taken sides with one or the other. But the majority of the common people are in favor of Jesus, believing him to be the Christ. The Pharisees most oppose him, because he boldly reproves their sins and hypocrisies.

Even Nicodemus, who at first was inclined to accept Jesus as a prophet, finding the Pharisees against him, and being unwilling to lose his popularity with them, kept away from the house where Jesus was by day; but his curiosity to learn more of him led him to visit the holy Prophet secretly by night. This he did twice, coming alone in the darkness, and being let in by his friend Rabbi Amos. What the results of these interviews was I can only tell you from Mary's account. She overheard their conversation, her window opening upon the corridor, where Jesus was seated after supper, alone in the moonlight, for full an hour, gazing meditatively heavenward. His pale and chiseled features in the white moonlight seemed radiant as marble, when Rabbi Amos came and announced the ruler, Nicodemus, as desirous of speaking with him.

"Bid him come in and see me, if he has aught to say to me," answered the Prophet, turning towards him.

"Nicodemus," added my Cousin Mary, "then came to the corridor, wrapped carefully in his mantle, and, looking about to see if he was unobserved, he dropped it from his face, and, bowing reverently, said to the Prophet:

"'Pardon me, O Rabbi, that I come to thee by night, but by day thy time is taken up with healing and teaching. I am glad to find thee alone, great Prophet, for I would ask thee many things.'

"'Speak, Nicodemus, and I will listen to thy words,' answered the Prophet.

"'Rabbi,' said the ruler of the Pharisees, 'I know thou art a teacher come from God, for no man can do these things that thou doest except God be with him. That thou art a mighty prophet I believe, as do all men; but art thou Messias? Tell us plainly. We read that Messias is to be a king who will rule the whole earth!'

"'My kingdom, O ruler of the Pharisees, is not of this world. I am indeed a king, but of a spiritual kingdom. My kingdom, unlike earthly kingdoms, has no end, and those who enter it must be born again. If not, they cannot see or desire this kingdom.'

"'Born again!' answered Nicodemus, with surprise: 'how can a man be born a second time? O Rabbi, thou speakest in parables!'

"'Verily, verily, I say unto thee,' answered the Prophet, 'except a man be born of water and of the Spirit, he cannot enter my kingdom. He that is born again is born a spiritual man and of my kingdom. Marvel not, then, that I say unto thee, ye must be born again.'

"When Nicodemus left him, Rabbi Amos said, 'Is it indeed true, O Master, that thou art to establish a kingdom?'

"'Yes, Rabbi Amos, a kingdom in which dwelleth righteousness,' answered the Prophet. 'Thou shalt yet behold me on my throne, O Amos, raised above the earth, and drawing all men unto me.'

"'Wilt thou have thy throne in the clouds of heaven, O Master, that thou shalt be raised above the earth upon it?' asked Rabbi Amos.

"'My throne shall be set on Calvary, and the ends of the earth shall look unto me and acknowledge my empire. Thou knowest not these things now, but hereafter thou shalt remember that I told thee of them.'"

Jesus then rose and, bidding his host good-night, retired to the apartment which was assigned him, and Mary remained wondering on his sayings.

Thus, dear father, it is made certain from his own words that Jesus is the Christ and that he is to establish a kingdom. But why his throne shall be on Calvary instead of Mount Zion, Rabbi Amos wonders greatly, for Calvary is a place of skulls and of public executions, and is covered with Roman crosses, where every week some malefactor is crucified for his crimes.

This morning, as Jesus was going forth from the house to depart into the country, a man lame from his youth, seated upon the threshold, caught him by the robe, saying, "Master, heal me!"

"Son, thy sins be forgiven thee!" answered Jesus, and then passed on; but the scribes and Pharisees who stood about cried, "This man, be he prophet or no, blasphemeth, for God alone can forgive sins!"

Jesus stopped and, turning to them, said:

"Which is easier, to say to this man, 'Thy sins be forgiven thee?' or to say, 'Rise and walk'? That ye may know that the Son of God hath power on earth to forgive sins—behold!"

Then in a loud voice the Prophet said to the lame man, "Arise, take up thy bed, and go to thine house!"

Immediately the man rose to his feet, leaping and praising God, and taking up the mattress upon which they had brought him to the door, he ran swiftly away to show himself to his kinsfolk, while all the people shouted and praised God.

Thus did Jesus publicly show men that he could forgive sins, if he could heal, as the power to do either came equally from God. Does not this power prove that he is the Son of God?

You should have seen him, dear father, as he left our house to go away into Galilee! The street was lined with all the afflicted of Jerusalem, and as he moved on between the rows of wretched sufferers, whose hollow eyes and shrivelled arms were turned imploringly towards him, he healed by words addressed to them, as he moved on, so that where he found disease before him, stretched on beds, he left behind him health and empty couches. We all wept at his departure and followed him to the Damascus Gate. Here there was assembled a large company of Levites and priests, among whom were mingled some of the most desperate characters in Jerusalem. Knowledge of this fact reached Rabbi Amos, who at once sent a message to Æmilius, our Roman friend, informing him that he apprehended that there would be an attempt made to assassinate Jesus at the going out of the gate, and asking his aid.

Æmilius placed himself at the head of fifty horse, and reaching the gate, pressed the crowd back, and took possession of it. When Jesus had passed through the armed guard beneath the arch, the young Roman courteously offered him an escort to the next village.

Æmilius, who informed me of these things, conducted him as far as Ephraim, and then was about to leave him to return to the city, when four lepers came from the cemetery of the tombs, near the village, and crying out afar off, said:

"Thou blessed Christ, have mercy on us!"

Jesus stopped and called to the lepers to approach. As they obeyed, the whole company of people, as well as the Roman soldiers, drew back to a distance, in horror at the sight of these dead-living men. They came timidly within twenty paces of Jesus and stood still tremblingly.

"Fear not," said he, "I will make you whole!"

He then advanced towards them, and laying his hand upon each of them, they all, at the touch, were instantly changed to well men, with the buoyant form, clear eye, and rich bloom of health.

When Æmilius saw this miracle, he dismounted from his horse, and falling at Jesus' feet, worshiped him.

Now, my dear father, I have thus far faithfully written all that I have heard and witnessed respecting Jesus, as you desire. You must see that he is more than a prophet, and must be the very Christ, the Son of the Blessed. Withhold, oh, withhold not your belief longer!

Your affectionate and loving daughter,

Adina.

LETTER XX.

My Dear Father:

We are now at the humble abode of Sarah, at Nain, whither I have come to breathe the fresh mountain air for a time. Her cottage stands in a garden, from which is a sublime view of Tabor, in all the majesty of his mountain grandeur. One day while I was in the garden walking, two men, dusty and travel-worn, stopped at the half-open gate, and saluting us, said:

"Peace be to this house, maiden, and all who dwell therein."

"Enter," said the widow, overhearing them, "enter and ye shall have water for your feet and bread for your hunger."

The two men then entered and seated themselves, and having been refreshed by the poor but hospitable widow, one of them rose and said:

"'This day is salvation come to this house. We are ambassadors of Jesus of Nazareth, and go from city to city, proclaiming the day of the Lord at hand, for Messiah is come!'"

"Will he, then, come to Nain?" asked the widow with emotion. "I should be willing to die so that I could lay my eyes once upon so great and holy a man!"

"Yes, he will come hither," answered the men, "and when we shall report to him your hospitality to us, he will visit your house, for he never forgets a cup of water given to one of his disciples."

The men then departed, again calling the peace of God upon our abode. They had not been gone many minutes before we heard a great commotion in the market-place near by. Upon going to the house-top, we beheld these two men standing upon an elevation, and preaching the kingdom of Christ at hand. Upon this, some cried out against Jesus, and others threw stones at the two men, and when we reached the house-top, we saw one of them remove his sandals and shake the dust from them, saying in a loud voice:

"As ye reject the words of life, your sins remain upon you, as I return to you the dust of your city."

They then departed, followed by Levites, who fairly drove them from the town.

While we were grieving at this enmity against a Prophet sent from God, whose life is a series of good deeds, there entered hastily a fair young maid whose name was Ruth. She held an open letter in her hand, and her beautiful face glowed rosily with some secret joy, which contrasted strangely with the present sadness of our own. We knew Ruth well, and loved her as if she had been a sister. She was an orphan, and dwelt with her uncle, Elihaz, the Levite, a man of influence in the town. She was artless, unsuspecting, and very interesting in all her ways.

"What good news, dear Ruth?" asked Mary, smiling in response to her bright smiles. "A letter from whom?"

"For Sarah," answered the pretty maid, blushing so timidly and consciously that we half suspected the truth.

"But that is not telling us from whom," persevered Mary, with a little playfulness.

"You can guess," she answered, glancing over her white shoulder, as she bounded away from us into the house.

We were soon after her, and heard her as she cried on putting the letter into the dear widow's hand:

"From Samuel!"

"God be blessed!" cried the widow. "My son liveth and is well!"

"Read, dear Sarah!" cried the maiden. "He was at Alexandria when he wrote this, and will soon be at home. Oh, happy, happy day!" added the overjoyed girl, quite forgetful of our presence.

"Nay," said the widow, "my eyes are filled with tears of gladness; I cannot see to read. Do thou read it aloud. Let Adina and Mary also know what he writeth."

Ruth then cast a bright look upon us, and read aloud the letter from over the sea, which told that the writer would return in the first ship bound to Sidon, or Cesarea, when he hoped to behold her and his mother face to face, and to receive as his bride the maiden he had so long loved and cherished in his heart.

At length, as the day drew near for me to leave, we were all filled with delightful surprise at the appearance of the long-absent son and lover in the midst of our happy circle.

Mary and I had once seen him, and we were now impressed with his manly and sun-browned beauty, his bold air, and frank, ingenuous manner. We could not but agree that the pretty Ruth had shown fine taste. But alas! my dear father, our joy was short-lived! Little did we anticipate how speedily our rejoicing was to end in mourning! The very night of his return he was seized with a malignant fever, which he had brought from Africa with him, and we were all overwhelmed with grief.

It would be impossible to paint the anguish of the mother, the heart-rending distress of his betrothed.

Unconscious of their presence, he raved wildly, and sometimes fancied himself suffering thirst on the burning sands of Africa, and at others battling with barbarians for his life. All that physicians could do was of no avail. This morning, the third day after his return, he expired, amid the most distressing agonies.

Alas! instead of a bridal, behold a funeral! Already the bearers are at the door, and in a few minutes he will be borne forth upon the dead-bier to the burial-place without the city.

"Oh!" sighs Mary near me as I write, "Oh, that Jesus, the mighty Prophet, had been here! He could have healed him!"

John has sent to her a message, saying that Jesus is traveling this way, on his mission of healing and teaching, and may be here this evening. But what will it avail, dear father? Even Jesus may not return the dead to life! Oh, if he could have been here yesterday, his power over disease would have enabled him to save this precious life!

I hear the heavy tread of the dead-bearers in the court below. The shrieks and wails of the mourning-women thrill my soul with awe. But above all pierces the wild cry of anguish of the bereaved mother! Ruth's voice is hushed. She has been for the last hour inanimate as marble. Only by her pulse can it be said she lives! Poor maiden! The blow is too terrible for her to bear.

My Cousin Mary has at this moment received a small roll of parchment which, from the flush on her cheek, I know to be from her betrothed. She smiles sadly, and with tears in her eyes hands it to me.

I have read it, dear father. It is as follows:

> "Gadara, beyond Judea.
>
> "The bearer, beloved, is one of the disciples of Jesus. His name is Bartimeus. He was blind and poor, and subsisted by begging; and, as you see, his sight is restored, and he insists now on going from town to town where he has been known as a blind man to proclaim what Jesus has done for him. This letter cometh beseeching thee, maiden, that as we love one another unfeignedly, so may we soon be united in that holy union which God hath blessed and

commanded. But, having much to say hereupon, I will not commit it to paper and ink; but by to-morrow, or the day after, I trust to come to you, and speak with you, dearly beloved, face to face, upon those things which now come to my lips. Farewell, lady. Peace be with you, and all in your house. Greet thy friends in my name, letting them know that we shall shortly be with you."

"Oh, that the mighty Prophet had come one day sooner!" cried Mary. "What woe and anguish would have been spared poor Ruth and his mother! But the will of Jehovah be done!"

We hear now, dear father, the voice of the governor of the funeral, bidding us come down to bury the dead.

Farewell, my father. I know you will shed a tear to the memory of the noble youth whose death has this day filled all Nain with mourning. As I look from the lattice, I see the concourse of people to be immense, filling all the street. Now, may the God of our father Abraham preserve and keep you, and suffer us once more to meet face to face in joy and peace.

Your dutiful and sorrowful daughter,

Adina.

LETTER XXI.

My Dear Father:

I seize my pen, which I laid down an hour ago in order to follow to his burial the son of our hostess, to recount to you one of the most extraordinary things which ever happened. I fear my trembling fingers will scarcely express legibly what I have to tell you.

When the burial train of Samuel had formed to go to the grave, the deep grief of poor Ruth overcame her wholly and I led her to her room, where she sank insensible upon her couch. I could not leave her in her situation, and the procession went forth from the house without me.

As the funeral train passed the lattice, it seemed endless, but at length it passed by, and I was left alone with the motionless Ruth. As I gazed on the marble countenance of the bereaved maiden, I could not but pray that she might never recover from her swoon, to revive to the bitter realization of her loss.

Suddenly I heard a great shout. I started and hastened to the lattice. It was repeated louder and with a glad tone. It seemed to come from beyond the city walls, and from a hundred voices raised in unison. I knew that the house-top overlooked the walls, and seeing Ruth moved not, I ascended rapidly to the parapet, the shouts and glad cries still increasing as I went up. Upon reaching the flat roof and stepping on the parapet, I saw coming along the street towards the house, with the speed of the antelope, Elec, our Gibeonite slave. He was waving his hands wildly, and crying out something which I could not distinctly hear. Behind him I saw two youths running also, appearing to be the bearers of some great tidings.

I knew something wonderful must have occurred, but could not divine what it could be. On looking towards the gate, from which direction the shouts at intervals continued to approach, I discovered on the hillside of the cemetery many people crowded together, and evidently surrounding some person in their midst, for the whole order of the procession was broken up. The bier I could not discern, nor could I comprehend how the solemnity of the march of the funeral train was suddenly changed to a confused multitude, rending the sky with loud acclamations. The whole body of people was pressing back towards the city. The persons whom I had first seen running along the street, now made themselves audible as they drew nigher.

"He is alive! He is alive!" shouted Elec.

"He has risen from the dead!" cried the young man next behind him.

"He lives, and is walking back to the city!" called the third.

"Who—who is alive?" I eagerly demanded of Elec, as he passed beneath the parapet. "What is this shouting, O Elec?"

He looked up to me with a face expressive of the keenest delight, mixed with awe, and said:

"Young Rabbi Samuel is come to life! He is no longer dead! You will soon see him, for they are escorting him back to the city, and everybody is mad with joy. Where is Ruth, the maiden? I am come to tell her the glorious news."

With emotion that I cannot describe, hardly believing what I heard, I hastened to Ruth, in order to prevent the effects of too sudden joy. Upon reaching the apartment, I found that the voice of Elec, who had shouted the news of which he was the bearer into her ears, had aroused her from her stupor of grief. She was looking at him wildly and incomprehensively. I ran to her, and folding her in my arms, said:

"Dear Ruth, there is news—good news! It must be true! Hear the shouts of gladness in all the town!"

"Lives!" she repeated, shaking her head. "No—no—no! Yes, there!" she said, raising her beautiful, glittering eyes to heaven and pointing upward.

"But on earth also!" cried Elec, with positiveness. "I saw him sit up, and heard him speak, as well as ever he was!"

"How was it? Let me know all!" I cried.

"How? Who could have done such a miracle but the mighty Prophet we saw at Jerusalem!" he answered.

"Jesus?" I exclaimed, with joy.

"Who else could it be. Yes, he met the bier just outside the— But here they come!"

Elec was interrupted in his narrative by the increased noise of voices in the streets and the tramp of hundreds of feet. The next moment the room was filled with a crowd of the most excited persons, some weeping, some laughing, as if beside themselves. In their midst I beheld Samuel walking, alive and well! his mother clinging to him, like a vine upon an oak.

"Where is Ruth?" he cried. "Oh, where is she! Let me make her happy with my presence!"

I gazed upon him with awe, as if I had seen a spirit.

Ruth no sooner heard his voice than she uttered a shriek of joy. "He lives—he indeed lives!" and springing forward, she was saved from falling to the ground by being clasped to his manly breast.

"Let us kneel and thank God!" he said.

For a few minutes the scene was solemn and touching beyond any spectacle ever exhibited on earth.

When he had performed this first sacred duty, he rose to his feet and received all our embraces. Hundreds came in to see his face, and every tongue was eloquent in praise of the power of Jesus.

"And where is the holy Prophet?" I asked of Mary. "Shall he be forgotten amid all our joy!"

"We thanked him there with all our hearts, and bathed his hands with tears of gratitude," she answered, "but when they would have brought him into the city in triumph he conveyed himself away in the confusion, and no one could see aught of him. But John, who was with him, told me he would come into the city after quiet was restored, by and by, and he would bring him to our abode."

"Oh, I shall then behold him and thank him also!" I cried. "Make known to me, Mary, the particulars of this wonderful miracle."

"As we went weeping forth," said Mary, "slowly following the bier, and had passed the gate, we saw coming along the path through the valley leading to Tabor, a party of twelve or thirteen men on foot. They were followed by a crowd of men, women and children from the country, and were so journeying that they would meet us at the crossing of the stone bridge. Hearing some one say aloud, 'It is the Prophet of Nazareth, with his disciples,' I looked earnestly forward, and joyfully recognized Jesus at their head, with John walking by his side.

"'Oh, that Jesus had been in Nain when thy son was sick!' I said to the widow, pointing him out to her, as he and his company stopped at the entrance to the bridge. Recollecting how he might have prevented her son's dying had he been in Nain, the poor lady could no longer command her grief, and covering her face with her veil, she wept so violently that all eyes were piteously fastened upon her. I observed that the holy Prophet's gaze rested upon her with compassion, and as she came opposite where he stood, he advanced towards us and said, in a voice of thrilling sympathy:

"'Weep not, mother. Thy son shall live again!'

"'I know it, O Rabboni, at the last day,' she answered. 'Oh, if thou hadst been here my son need not have died! Thy word would have healed him! But now he is dead! dead! dead!'

"'Woman, weep not! I will restore thy son!'

"'What saith he?' cried some Pharisees who were in the funeral. 'That he will raise a dead man? This is going too far. God only can raise the dead.' And they smiled and scoffed.

"But Jesus laid his hand upon the pall over the body, and said to those who bore the corpse:

"'Rest the bier upon the ground.'

"They instantly stood still and obeyed him. He then advanced amid a hushed silence, and uncovering the marble visage, touched the hand of the dead young man, and said, in a loud and commanding voice:

"'Young man, I say unto thee, Arise!'

"There was a moment's painful stillness through the vast multitude. Every eye was fixed upon the bier. The voice was heard by the spirit of the dead and it came back to his body. There was at first visible a living, trembling emotion of the hitherto motionless corpse! Color flushed the livid cheek; the eyelids opened and he fixed his eyes on Jesus; then he raised his hand and his lips moved! The next moment he sat up on the bier, and spake aloud in his natural voice, saying:

"'Lo, here I am!'

"Jesus then took him by the hand, and assisting him to alight upon his feet from the bier, led him to his mother, and delivered him to her, saying:

"'Woman, behold thy son!'

"Upon seeing this miracle the people shouted with joy and wonder, 'God has indeed visited his people Israel! A great Prophet is risen up among us! The Messias is come, and Jesus is the very Christ, with the keys of death and hell!'

"I sought out Jesus to cast myself at his feet, but he shrunk from the homage and gratitude which his mercy to us had awakened. Thus humility is an element of all power."

Such, my dear father, is the narrative of the restoration to life again of Samuel, the son of Sarah, widow of Nain. This miracle has caused hundreds this day to confess his name, and to believe in Jesus as the anointed Shiloh of Israel.

Many of the doctors have been to see Samuel through the day, and have put profound questions to him touching the state of the soul out of the body, but he could give them no satisfaction, all appearing to him like shining fragments of a gorgeous vision.

Mary is to-morrow to become the bride of John, and Jesus will be present at the wedding, for while he severely rebukes sin and folly, he sanctifies by his presence the holy rite of marriage.

On the eve of the eighth day from this I shall depart hence, with John and Mary, for Jerusalem, whence I will write you again.

Your loving daughter,

Adina.

LETTER XXII.

Once more, my dear father, I address a letter to you from this holy city. This morning when I awoke at the sound of the silver trumpets of the priests, ringing melodiously from the top of Mount Moriah, I experienced anew that profound devotion which the children of Abraham must always feel in the city of God and in the presence of his very Temple.

It was a joyous morning to me, dear father, for Æmilius, the noble Roman Prefect, was this day voluntarily to present himself at the Temple to be made a proselyte to the holy faith of Israel.

The morning was, therefore, additionally lovely to me. I thought I had never seen the olive groves on the hillside beyond the king's gardens so green, nor the harvest so yellow, as they undulated in the soft breeze of the opening morn. The lofty palms everywhere appeared to bend and wave their verdant fans with joyous motion. The birds in the palace gardens sang sweeter and louder, and Jerusalem itself seemed more beautiful than ever.

While I was gazing upon the scene and adoring God, and thanking him for the conversion of Æmilius, Rabbi Amos came and said that he would take us to the Temple. We were soon on our way, climbing the paved pathway to Moriah. Oh, how sublimely towered the divine Temple above our heads, seemingly lost in the blue of the far heaven! The great gates opening north and south, to the east and west, were thronged with the multitude pressing through; while from the galleries above each gate pealed forth continually the clear-voiced trumpets of God in ceaseless reverberation. My uncle pointed out to me the massive doors, all overlaid with sheets of beaten gold, and the floor of green marble on which we trod. He bade me notice the costly entablature of colored stones, exquisitely worked with the Grecian's chisel, and especially the roof of fretted silver, set with precious stones, the onyx, beryl, sapphire, carbuncle and jasper. I was dazzled by the magnificence, and awed by the vast extent of the space of splendor surrounding me, while ten thousands of people were to be seen moving towards the altar of sacrifice. From that superb court I was led into a hall nearly a hundred cubits in length, its ceiling of pure gold sustained by a thousand and one columns of porphyry and white marble, ranged alternately.

I was not permitted to approach the sacred chamber, where stood the four thousand vessels of gold of Ophir, used in the sacrifices on great days; and this being a high day, I saw no less than six hundred priests standing about the altar, each with a golden censer in his hand. Beyond is the holy ark of the covenant, over which the cherubim hover, their wings meeting, and between them is the mercy-seat. As this was the Holy of Holies I was not permitted to see it; but its position was pointed out to me within the veil, which conceals from all eyes but that of the High Priest once a year the place of God's throne on the earth, alas now left vacant since the glory of the Shechinah departed from the Holy of Holies!

The air of the vast Temple was delicious with the fragrance of burning frankincense. As the victims bled and the smoke ascended, the people fell on their faces and worshiped God. After a few moments' silence, a startling trumpet note thrilled every soul in the countless multitude. It was followed by a peal of music that shook the air, from a choir of two thousand singers, male and female, of the sons and daughters of Levi, who served in the Temple. Entering from the southern court, they advanced in long procession, singing sacred chants, and playing on sacbut and harp, psalter and nebble, chinna and tympana. As they ascended to the choir their voices, mingling with the instruments, filled all the Temple. I never heard before such sublime harmony; especially when on reaching the elevated choir, a thousand Levites with manly voices joined them, and the whole company chanted one of the sublimest of the Psalms of David.

When the chant was concluded, the whole multitude responded, "Amen and Amen!" like the deep voice of a mighty wind suddenly shaking the foundations of the Temple.

At length I beheld a train of priests following the High Priest, as he marched thrice around the altar. In that procession I discovered a company of proselytes, escorted by twelve aged Levites, with long, snowy beards, and clad in vestments of the purest white. Among the proselytes I discerned the tall and noble figure of the Roman Æmilius. He was robed in a black garment from head to foot. But upon approaching the baptismal basin two young priests removed this outer sable dress and robed him in white. I then saw him baptized into the family of Abraham and a new name given him, that of Eleazer. I heard the silver trumpets proclaim the conversion and the multitude shouting their joy.

Of the rest of the ceremony I have no recollection, as after the baptism of Æmilius, I was too happy to see or think of anything else.

While I was lifting up my heart in gratitude for the happy conversion of Æmilius, and while the Jews were crowding about him to extend to him the hand of fellowship, rejoicing that so noted a person should embrace our faith, Uncle Amos drew my attention by exclaiming with gladness:

"Behold, there is Jesus, the Prophet!"

We at once made our way, but with difficulty, towards the spot where we had discovered him. The rumor that the Christ was in the Temple rapidly spread, and the whole multitude pressed towards the same point. At length we obtained our object so as to get within a few feet of him. Here a tall, richly-attired Greek addressed Rabbi Amos, saying:

"Sir, tell me who that youthful Jew is, whose countenance is stamped with firmness and benevolence so finely combined in its expression; whose air possesses such dignity and wisdom; whose noble eyes seem filled with a holy sadness, and whose glance is full of innocence and sweetness. He seems born to love men and to command them. All seek to approach him. Pray, sir, who is he?"

"That, O stranger, is Jesus of Nazareth, the Jewish Prophet," answered Uncle Amos, delighted to point him out to a foreigner.

"Then I am well rewarded for my journey in turning aside to Jerusalem," answered the Grecian. "I have even heard of his fame in Macedonia, and am rejoiced to behold him. Think you he will do some great miracle?"

"He performs miracles not to gratify curiosity but to bear testimony to the truths he teaches, that they are delivered to him of God. Hark! He speaks!" cried my uncle.

Every voice was hushed as that of Jesus rose clear and sweet, and thrilling like a celestial clarion speaking. And he preached, dear father, a sermon so full of wisdom, of love to man, of love to God, of knowledge of our hearts, of divine and convincing power, that thousands wept; thousands were chained to the spot with awe and delight, and all were moved as if an angel had addressed them. They cried, "Never man spake like this man!"

The priests, seeing that he had carried the hearts of all the people, were greatly enraged, and, not being able to vent their hatred and fear in any other way, they hired a vile person by the name of Gazeel, a robber who, taking one of the blood-stained sacrificing knives by the altar, crept towards him behind the column, and, securing a favorable position to execute the deed, raised his hand to strike the Prophet from behind, when Jesus, turning his head, arrested the hand of the assassin in mid-air by a look. Unable to move a muscle, Gazeel stood betrayed to all eyes in this murderous attitude, like a statue of stone.

"Return to those who hired thee. My hour is not yet come, nor can they yet have any power over me."

The assassin bowed his head in abject shame and terror; the knife dropped from his hand and rang upon the marble floor, and he sank at Jesus' feet imploring forgiveness. The people would instantly have torn Gazeel in pieces, but Jesus said:

"Let him depart in peace. The day shall come when he will be willing to lay down his life to save mine. Ye priests go about to kill me," he added, fixing his clear gaze upon the group which had sent Gazeel. "For what do ye seek my life? I have come to my own, and to my Temple, and ye receive me not. The day cometh when this Temple shall be thrown down, and not one stone left upon another; and some who hear me shall behold and mourn in that day. Oh, Jerusalem, thou that killest the prophets, and stonest them that are sent unto thee, how oft would I have gathered thy children together as a hen gathereth her chickens under her wings, and ye would not. Thou shalt be left desolate and cast out among cities, because thou knewest not the day of thy visitation. Fly ye to the Jerusalem which is above, and which is above all, whose foundation is eternal, and whose Temple is the Lord God Almighty, who is also the light and glory thereof."

Upon hearing these words, there arose a great cry from ten thousand voices:

"Hail to Jesus, the king of Israel and Judah! Hosanna to the Prince of David! We will have no king but Jesus!"

At this shout, which was caught up and repeated beyond the four gates of the Temple, the priests cried aloud that the people were in insurrection.

Pilate, who was, with his guard, just leaving the Court of the Gentiles, hearing it, turned to ask what it meant. One of the priests, desirous of having Jesus slain, quickly answered, "That the people had proclaimed Jesus, the Nazarene, king."

Hearing this, Pilate sent off messengers to the Castle of David for soldiers, and with his body-guard turned back to the Temple gate, charging the people sword in hand.

The tumult was now fearful, and the bloodshed would have been great, but Jesus suddenly appeared before him—none saw how he had reached the place—and said:

"O Roman, I seek no kingdom but such as my Father hath given me. My kingdom is not of this world."

Pilate was seen to bend his proud head with low obeisance before the Prophet, and said graciously:

"I have no wish to arrest thee. Thy word, O Prophet, is sufficient for me. Of thee I have hitherto heard much. Wilt thou come with me to my palace, and let me hear thee, and see some miracle?"

"Thou shalt see me in thy palace, but not to-day; and thou shalt behold a miracle, but not now."

When Jesus had thus said, he withdrew himself from Pilate's presence; and those who would have sought him to make him a king could nowhere discover him.

The result of this attempt of the people to make the Prophet their king, and under his direction to overthrow the Roman power, is that the Roman authorities, instigated by Annas and the priests, look upon Jesus with eyes of jealousy, and Pilate this morning told a deputation of priests, who waited on him to petition him to arrest and imprison the Prophet, that on the first proof they could bring him of his hostility to Cæsar he would send soldiers to take him. To-day Jesus was refreshing himself in our house, when several Scribes and Pharisees came in. I saw by their dark looks they meditated evil, and secretly sent Elec with a message to Æmilius (now Eleazer) asking him to be at hand to protect Jesus; for Æmilius is devoted to him, as we are, and Jesus takes delight in teaching him the things of the kingdom of God.

Jesus, knowing the hearts of these bad men, said to them, after they had seated themselves and remained some minutes in silence:

"Wherefore are ye come?"

"Master," said Zadoc, a Levite of great fame among the people, "we have heard how boldly thou speakest at all times; that not even Pilate, nor Herod, yea, nor Cæsar, could make thee refrain from what thou choosest to utter. Is it lawful for us Jews, the peculiar nation of God, to pay tribute to Cæsar, who is an idolater? Is it lawful for us to obey the laws of Pilate, rather than of Moses? We ask this as Jews to a Jew. Tell us frankly."

Jesus looked fixedly upon them, as if he read their wicked designs, and said:

"Show me the tribute money."

Zadoc handed him a penny, the Roman coin sent into Judea by Cæsar, as our currency, and which we return to Rome again in tribute. When Jesus had taken the money, he looked at the head of Augustus stamped upon one side, and then turning to them, said:

"Whose image and whose name is here impressed?"

"Cæsar's," eagerly answered the whole party.

"Then render unto Cæsar the things that be Cæsar's, and unto God the things that be God's," was his calm and wonderful answer.

I breathed again, for I feared he would answer openly that tribute ought not to be paid, which they hoped he would do, when they would immediately have accused him to Pilate as teaching that we ought not to pay tribute to Rome, and so fomenting rebellion.

But the divine wisdom of his answer relieved all our minds; while the Scribes and Levites, his enemies, looked upon him with amazement, interchanged glances of conscious defeat, and left the house.

I remain your affectionate daughter,

Adina.

LETTER XXIII.

My Dear Father:

I have received with joy your letter, in which you say you shall leave Egypt with the next Passover caravan, in order to visit Jerusalem. My happiness is augmented to know that you will be here while Jesus is in the city; for it is said, and John, Mary's husband, asserts, that he will certainly be at the Passover.

Last week Eli, the paralytic, whom you knew, a scribe of the Levites, whose hand has been withered nine years, so that he had been dependent on the alms of the worshipers in the Temple for his bread, hearing of the power of Jesus, sought him at the house of Uncle Amos, where he was abiding.

Jesus was reclining with our family at the evening meal, at the close of the day on which the uproar had taken place in the Temple, when Eli came and stood within the door. Humble and doubting, his knees trembled, and he timidly and wistfully looked towards Jesus, but did not speak. I knew at once what the afflicted man came for, and approached him, saying, "Fear not, Eli; ask him, and he will make thee whole!"

Jesus did not see the poor man, his face being turned towards Rabbi Amos; but leaving this conversation, he said in a gentle voice, without turning round:

"Come to me, Eli, and ask what is in thy heart. And fear not; for if thou believest, thou shalt receive all thy wish."

At this Eli ran forward, and casting himself at Jesus' feet, kissed them and said, "Rabboni, I am a poor, sinful man; I believe that thou art the Christ, the Son of the Blessed!"

"Dost thou believe, Eli, that I have power to make thee whole?" asked Jesus, looking steadily upon him.

"I believe, my Lord," answered Eli, bowing his face to the ground.

"Thy sins, then, be forgiven thee. Rise and go to thy house; and sin no more, lest a worse thing come upon thee."

"This man! forgiveth he sins also?" cried a venerable priest, Manasses, who was at the table. "He is a blasphemer! for God alone forgiveth sins. Will he call himself God?" And he rose quickly up and rent his robe, and spat upon the floor in detestation.

"Manasses," said Jesus mildly, "tell me whether it is an easier thing to do—to say unto this man kneeling here, 'Thy sins be forgiven thee?' or to say, 'Stretch forth thine hand whole as the other'?"

"It would be more difficult to do the latter," answered Manasses, surprised at the question. "God alone, who made him, can do that."

Jesus turned to the paralytic. "I say unto thee, Eli, stretch forth thy hand whole!"

The man, looking upon Jesus' face, and seeming to derive confidence from its expression of power, made a convulsive movement with his arm, which was bared to the shoulder, exhibiting all its hideous deformity, and stretched it forth at full length. Immediately the arm was rounded with flesh and muscles; the pulse filled and leaped with the warm life-blood, and it became whole as the other. The change was so instantaneous that it was done before we could see how it was done. The amazed and wonderingly delighted Eli bent his elbow, and expanded and contracted the fingers, felt the flesh and pressed it with his other hand, before he could realize he was healed. Then, casting himself at the feet of the Prophet, he cried:

BETHANY

"Thou art not a man, but Gabriel, the angel of God!"

"Thou art now healed, Eli," said Jesus impressively. "Worship God, and go and sin no more."

Who, dear father, but Messias could do this miracle? My mind is overwhelmed—I am filled with astonishment and awe, when I reflect upon the might, power and majesty of Jesus, and I fear to ask myself. Who more than man is he? Is he verily the awful and terrible Jehovah of Sinai, visible in the human form? Oh, wondrous and incomprehensible mystery! I dare not trust my thoughts to penetrate the mystery in which he walks among us in the veiled Godhead of his power. His beloved disciple, John, said that Jesus has told him the day is not far off when this veil will be removed, and when we shall then know him, who he is, and wherefore he has come into the world, and the infinite results to men of his mission.

Your devoted daughter,

Adina.

LETTER XXIV.

My Dear Father:

As I was closing my last letter to you, intelligence reached my Uncle Amos that Lazarus, the amiable brother of Martha and Mary, was very ill. The message was brought by Elec, the Gibeonite slave, who, with tears in his eyes, communicated to us the sad news. My Cousin Mary and I at once set out to Bethany with him.

"Knowest thou, Elec, the disease that has so suddenly seized my cousin?" asked Mary, as we wound slowly up the path that leads around the steepest side of Olivet.

"Ah, dear me, noble lady, I know not," answered Elec, shaking his head. "He had just returned from the city, where he had been staying night and day for a week, laboring industriously to complete a copy of the five books of the blessed Moses for the Procurator's chief captain, for which he was to receive a large sum in Roman gold."

"What was the name of this captain who seeks to obtain our holy books?" I asked, hope half answering the question in my heart.

"Æmilius, the brave knight, they say, who was made a proselyte at the last Passover."

I was rejoiced to hear this proof of the steady desire of the princely Roman knight to learn our sacred laws, you may be assured, dearest father. But Elec went on speaking and said:

"It was his hard work to complete this copy which made him ill; for he slept not, nor ceased to toil until he had completed it, and when he came home with the silver-bound roll in his hand, and laid it upon the table before his sisters, he fell at the same moment fainting to the ground."

"Alas, poor Lazarus!" we both exclaimed, and urged our mules forward at a faster pace, our hearts bleeding for the sorrow of his sisters and for his sad condition.

At length, half an hour after leaving the gate of the city, we drew near to Bethany, and beheld the roof of the house of Lazarus. Upon it, watching the road towards Jerusalem for us, we discovered the graceful form of Mary. In a few moments we were in her arms, mingling our tears together.

"Does he yet live?" I asked, scarcely daring to inquire, as she led us into the house.

"Yes, lives, but fails hourly," answered Mary, with forced composure. "God bless you both for hastening to me."

At this moment Martha's pale and suffering face, beautiful even in its pallor, appeared in the door of the inner room. Upon seeing us she advanced, and taking both our hands in hers, said in a touching whisper, "You have come, sweet friends, to see my brother die!"

She then led us into the room, where lay upon a couch the form of the invalid.

"He has slept a little," said Martha softly to me, "but his fever is consuming him. He has now closed his eyes again and seems heavy, but his slumbers are restless, as you see, and he seems to think his dear friend, Jesus the Prophet, is by him; or he talks of Rachel as if she were not present."

"And who is Rachel, dear Martha?" I asked, as I was about to follow her out of the room, leaving her brother to his weary repose.

"Alas! It was for Rachel's gentle love's sake he now lies there," she answered. "There is the sweet maiden kneeling on the other side of his couch, her tearful face buried in the folds of the curtains."

I turned and regarded with tender interest the graceful and half-concealed form of the young girl as she bent over his pillow, her hand clasped by his. At this moment she looked up and directed her gaze towards me. Her face was inexpressibly lovely, bathed as it was in its glittering tear-dews, and her large, glorious eyes shone like starry heavens of tenderness and love. Her hair would have been raven black, save that rays of golden bronze enriched its waving masses with every play of the light upon it. As our eyes met, she seemed to receive me into her soul, and my heart to embrace hers. Lazarus now moved and murmured her name, when she dropped her eyes and bent like an angel over him.

"Who is this marvelously lovely maiden?" I asked of Martha, as we went into the court of the hall.

"The betrothed bride of our beloved brother," answered she. "Sit with me here in the shade beneath this vine, and I will tell thee their sad story. Lazarus, you know, dearest Adina, is a writer in the Temple, and by his labors has surrounded us all with many comforts, nay, luxuries. His attachment to us led him to forego the pleasure of all other society, as he said he found in our sweet bond of sisterly love all that he required to render him happy.

"But a few weeks ago, as he was engaged late and alone in the copying-room of the Temple upon a roll which the noble Æmilius had ordered, he was startled by the sudden entrance of a young girl in great terror, who seemed to be flying from pursuit. Upon beholding him she bounded towards him, and casting herself at his feet, implored his protection. Amazed and interested, he promptly promised it, but had hardly spoken the words before Annas entered and advanced towards her. His face was flushed with rage, and his voice was loud and fierce as he demanded her at the hand of my brother.

"'Nay, my Lord Annas,' answered Lazarus, boldly, 'were a dove to seek shelter from a hawk in my bosom I would protect it, much more a distressed maiden of the daughters of Abraham!' and he placed himself before the fugitive.

"'Darest thou protect from me? She is my child, a wicked and disobedient daughter of Belial! Resign her to me, young scrivener, or I will have thee sent to the lowest dungeon of the Castle of David!'

"'Oh, save me! save me!' cried the young girl, as Annas advanced to seize her. 'I am not his child! I am the orphan of Rabbi Levi, who left me and my estate to this false priest as a sacred charge. He would now sell me in unholy marriage to a Greek captain in the Roman legion, who offers him large bribes in gold for me. Rather than be given into the hands of this fierce and terrible Grecian, I will cast myself down from the height of the Temple!'

"And to the surprise and horror of Lazarus, she bounded from the lattice and stood upon the edge of the rock, which looks sheer three hundred feet down into the valley beneath.

"'Thou seest, O Annas, to what thy cupidity for gold will drive this maiden. Has the land of Israel sunk so low that its chief priest will sell the daughters of the land for gold to the lust of the Gentiles? Is this the way thou givest protection to orphans? Leave her, and until I find a protector for her, she shall be a sacred guest with my sisters in their humble abode!'

"'Thy life shall pay for this arrogance, young man!' answered the priest. 'I have power and will exercise it.'

"'Not to the danger and wrong of this maiden, my Lord Annas, whom Jehovah will protect, since she has trustingly sought the sheltering wing of his altars,' answered my brother firmly. 'If thou continue to persecute her, I will appeal to the Procurator, Pontius Pilate, against thee.'

"The result was," continued Martha, "that the wicked priest, alarmed by the threat of appeal to Pilate, relinquished his present purpose and left them, breathing menaces against my brother. The same day Lazarus conducted the maiden, whom you already guess to be Rachel, to our house. She has since then been our guest, and has won all our hearts, as well as our dear brother's."

"Is there no hope for him?" I asked, after listening to her touching narrative.

"None; the physicians say that he will never rise again."

"There is one hope left," I said eagerly.

"What is that?" demanded Martha.

"Jesus!" I answered. "Send to him, O Martha, and he will yet save him, and raise him up to life and health."

I had no sooner spoken than Mary, who overheard me, uttered a cry of joy.

"Yes, Jesus has the power to heal him, and Jesus loves him! He will come and save him the moment he hears of his danger."

Immediately Mary wrote on a slip of parchment these brief and touching words:

"Lord, behold, he whom thou lovest is sick. Hasten to come to us, that he may live; for nothing is impossible with thee."

This message was forthwith despatched by the hands of a young friend to Bethabara, beyond Jordan, where we learned Jesus at present abides. We have, therefore, no hope for our dear relative but in the power of the Prophet. I will write as soon as we hear. I remain, dear father,

Your attached daughter,

Adina.

LETTER XXV.

My Dear and Honored Father:

It is with emotions of the deepest grief that I convey to you the sad intelligence of the death of Lazarus. The hand of the Lord hath fallen heavily upon this household and stricken down its prop; smitten the oak around which clung these vine-like sisters, vine-like in their dependence upon him and confiding trust in his wisdom and love. Now prostrate in the dust they lie stunned by the sudden and mysterious stroke of God's providence.

I have told you, dear father, something of this family; what a happy household I have seen it when Jesus completed the number; for he stayed so much with them when not preaching, or when wishing to rest a day or two from his weary toil, that they came to regard him as one of their family. Martha seemed ever to be thinking what and how she should administer to his comfort, by providing every delicacy for her table; but so that Jesus could find listeners to his words of truth and wisdom, like Mary—who loved to sit at his feet and hear the golden language fall from his sacred lips—he thought not of meat or drink.

One day when I, with Mary and Lazarus, was listening to his heavenly teachings, wrapt in wonder and absorbing interest, Martha, who was preparing the meal, came and desired Mary to come and assist her; but the dear, pious girl heeded not nor heard her, feeding, forgetful of all else, upon the celestial food that fell from the lips of Jesus. At length Martha, finding that Mary had not heard, appealed to Jesus, saying somewhat sharply:

"Lord, dost thou not care that my sister hath left me to serve alone? Bid her, therefore, that she help me."

We turned with surprise to hear her, who was usually so gentle and good, thus forget what was due to the presence of the Prophet, and Lazarus was about to speak and excuse his sister, who looked as if she were much worried with her domestic troubles, when Jesus said kindly to her:

"Martha, Martha, thou art careful and troubled about many things. But one thing is needful, and Mary hath chosen that good part, which shall not be taken away from her. While thou carest much for the wants of the body, she careth for those of the spirit. Think not, beloved Martha, of sumptuous living for me, who have no earthly goods, nor even where to lay my head."

"Say not thus, oh, say not so, dear Lord!" cried Martha, suddenly bursting into tears at Jesus' touching words, and casting herself impulsively at his feet. "This house is thy home—ever beneath its roof, while I have one above me, shalt thou have where to lay thy head; say not so, my Lord!"

We were all moved at Martha's pathetic earnestness. Jesus raised her up and said gently:

"It is thy love for me, I well know, that maketh thee so careful and troubled to provide for me at thy bountiful table. But I have meat to eat that ye know not of. To teach the truths of God, as thou findest me doing to these, is to me meat and drink, for therein I am doing my Father's will, who sent me."

My last letter closed with informing you of the departure of the messenger to Jesus. After he had gone out of sight from the door, and the last echo of his horse's hoofs ceased to be heard by the long-listening ears of his sister Martha, I re-entered the room where Lazarus lay. He was as white as marble. His large black eyes seemed to be twice their usual size and brilliancy. He breathed with difficulty, and every few moments he would be compelled to have his head raised in order to free his mouth from the welling blood that was constantly bubbling up from the broken fountains of his life. Mary's tender privilege it was, assisted by Rachel, to render him this service of love. As she bent over him, looking downward with anxious fondness into his pale, intellectual face, watching every shadow of the change that the sable wing of advancing Death cast over it, I thought I had never gazed on a more lovely being. I forgot for the moment the dying young man about whose form her snow-white arms were entwined, his head reclining upon her bosom, her raven tresses, bronzed with a changing light, all unbound and floating above him and over his pillow, like a rich veil interwoven of sable silken floss and threads of gold.

I commenced this letter by informing you of the departure of the good and generous and pious Lazarus. He fell asleep in death as an infant sinks to slumber in its mother's arms.

All too late was Jesus sent for! To-morrow his burial will take place. Alas, how suddenly has perished the noblest young man in Judea!

Farewell, dear father. My heart is full. I can now write no more. The God of Abraham preserve you in your journey, and bring you in safety to the embraces of

Your loving daughter,

Adina.

LETTER XXVI.

My Dear Father:

In my last letter I told you that Lazarus was dead. I write this to say that he who was dead is alive! Lazarus lives! He whom I saw dead and buried, and sealed up within the rocky cave of the tomb, is alive again from the dead; and at this moment, while I am penning this extraordinary account, I hear his voice from the porch.

How, my dear father, how shall I find adequate language to tell you all that has happened here within the last twenty-four hours!

The funeral procession was so very long that strangers, pausing, asked what great master in Israel, or person of note, was being taken to the sepulchre.

Some answered, "Lazarus, the industrious scribe;" others said, "A young man who has devoted his life to honor his mother." Others answered, as Lazarus himself, were he alive, would have had them:

"It is Lazarus, the friend of Jesus."

The place where they were to lay him was the cave in which his father and mother were entombed. It was in a deep, shady vale, thickly shaded by cypress, palm and pomegranate trees, and a large tamarind grew, with its stately branches, overclasping the summit of the secluded place of sepulchre. The remote swell of a Roman bugle from the head of a cohort, which was just issuing from a defile, came softly and musically to our ears, as we stood in silence about the grove wherein we were to place the dead. Æmilius, my betrothed, was also present, wearing a white scarf above his silver cuirass, in token of grief, for he also loved Lazarus. Of him, dear father, I have not of late spoken, for should I begin to write of him I should have no room in my letters for any other theme.

The sacred observances at the grove being over, they raised the body of the dead young man from the bier, and four youths, aided by Æmilius at the head to support it, conveyed it into the yawning cavern. A moment they lingered on the threshold, that Mary and Martha might take one more look, imprint upon its icy cold lips one last kiss, press once more his unconscious head to their loving and bursting hearts.

The young men moved slowly forward into the gloom of the cave. Mary rushed in, and with disheveled hair, cried:

"Oh, take him not away forever from the sight of my eyes! Oh, my brother, my brother, would that I had died for thee! for I am willing to lie down with the worm and call it my sister, and sleep in the arms of death, as on the breast of my mother, so thou couldst live! Oh, brother, brother, let them not take thee forever from the sight of my eyes! Without thee, how shall life be life!"

Rolling stone, closing a sepulchre.

Æmilius entered the tomb and, tenderly raising her from the body, on which she had cast herself in the eloquent abandonment of her wild grief, he led her forth, and beckoning to me, placed her in my arms.

The body, being placed in a niche hollowed out in the rock, was decently covered with a grave mantle, all but the calm face, which was bound about by a snow-white napkin. Maidens of the village advanced and cast flowers upon his head, and many, many were the sincere tears, both from beneath manly lids and those of virgins, which bore tribute to his worth.

The burial ceremonies being ended, five strong men replaced the ponderous stone door closely fitting the entrance to the cave, and so secured it, by letting it into a socket, that it would require a like number to remove it.

As they were retiring with heavy hearts from performing this last duty to the beloved dead, the sun sank beyond the blue hills of Ajalon in the west in a lake of gold. To enjoy the sunset, and to relieve our emotions of sadness, I walked apart with Mary to the top of the hill, from which I beheld the sun gilding the pinnacle of the Temple, and making it appear like a gigantic spear elevated into the sky. From the Levites at evening sacrifice came, mellowed by distance, the deep chant of the Temple service, uttered by a thousand voices. The cloud from the altar sacrifice ascended slowly into the still air, and catching the splendor of the sun's last beams, shone as if the pillar of cloud and of fire which stood above the tabernacle in the wilderness. The laborers in the harvest were hastening towards the gates, ere they should be shut out for the night by the Roman guards, and dwellers in the village were hurrying forth, lest they should be held in the city over night.

There was a sacred hush in the sleepy atmosphere that seemed in sympathy and touching harmony with the scene in which we had just borne a part. With Mary leaning sobbing upon my shoulder, I sat upon a rock giving my heart up to the sweet influences of the hour. We were alone, save Æmilius, who had ridden after us, anxious for our safety, and who sat upon his horse near by, gazing upon the beauty of the evening scene.

"I am calmer now," said Mary, after a while, raising her head and looking into my face, her splendid eyes glittering brimful with tears. "The peace of the sweet, holy skies seems to have descended and entered my heart. The spirit of Lazarus pervades all and hallows all I see. I will weep no more. He is happy now, very happy, and let us try to be holy and go to him, for he cannot come back to us."

At this moment we heard the tramp of horses' hoofs. Æmilius, startled thereby from his reverie, recovered his seat and laid his hand upon his sword. The next moment, around a rock projecting from the shoulder of Olivet, appeared a horseman in the wild, warlike costume of an Ishmaelite of the desert, brandishing a long spear in the air; then another and another similarly clad and armed, and mounted on superb horses of the desert, dashed in sight. These were immediately followed by a tall, daring-looking young man, in a rich costume, half Grecian, half Arabic, though his dark, handsome features were decidedly Israelitish. He rode a superb Abyssinian charger, and sat upon his back like the heathen centaur I have read of in the Latin books which Æmilius has given me to read. Upon seeing us he drew rein and smiled, and waved his jewelled hand with splendid courtesy; but at the sight of Æmilius his dark eyes flashed, and leaping to his feet in his stirrups he shook his glittering falchion towards him, and rode with a trumpet-like cry full upon him.

The brave Roman soldier received the charge by turning his horse slightly, and catching the point of the weapon upon the blade of his short sword.

"We meet at last, O Roman!" cried this wild, dashing chief, as he wheeled his horse like lightning, and once more rode upon the iron-armed Roman knight.

"Ay, Barabbas, and with joy I hail thee!" responded Æmilius, placing a bugle to his lips.

At hearing the clear voice of the bugle awaking the echoes of Olivet, the dread robber chief said haughtily and with a glance of contempt:

"Thou, a knight of the tribune, and commander of a legion, call for aid, when I offer thee equal battle, hand to hand, and ask not for aid of my own men's spears?"

"I know no equal battle with a robber. I would hunt thee as I would do the wolf and the wild beasts of thy deserts," answered Æmilius, pressing him closely. At a signal from the robber chief his four men, who had reined up a short distance off, near the tomb of Lazarus, sent up a shrill, eaglelike scream, that made my blood stand still, and then rode down like the wind to overcome Æmilius.

Hitherto I had remained as one stupefied at being an involuntary spectator of a sudden battle, but on seeing his danger, I was at his side, scarce knowing how I reached the place.

"Retire, dear Adina," he said authoritatively. "I shall have to defend both thee and myself, and these barbarians will give both my hands enough to do."

As he spoke he turned his horse's head to meet the forefold shock, and I escaped, I know not how, with the impulse to hasten to Bethany for succor. But heaven interposed its aid. A detachment of the body-guard of Pilate, hearing the recall of their chief's bugle, came now cantering up the hill. At the sight Barabbas and his party fled, like wild pigeons pursued by a cloud of Iturean hawks. Barabbas, however, turned more than once to fling back defiance to his foes. Æmilius soon reached his side, seized the crimson sash which encircled his waist, and held him thus, both fighting as they rode. The Roman troop came up, and after a desperate battle the celebrated chief was taken alive, though bleeding with many wounds, and bound with his own sash to the column of one of the tombs.

Æmilius says that Barabbas will assuredly be crucified for his numerous crimes. Dreadful punishment! and for one so young as this desert robber to come to such an ignominious and agonizing death; doomed to hang for hours under the sunbeams by his lacerated hands and feet, till death at last comes from slow exhaustion of all the powers of nature. I am amazed that so polite and humane a nation as the Roman can inflict such a cruel and agonizing death, even upon their malefactors. Ignominious, indeed, must the life of a man have been, for him to be doomed justly to suffer such a death.

In this letter, dearest father, I intended to relate to you how Lazarus has been restored to life, but it is already taken up with so much, that I defer it to my next. Suffice it for me to tell you at the close of this letter that it was Jesus who raised him from the dead. And will you say that he is an impostor? That he has done this wonderful thing is alone evidence enough to me that he is indeed the Messias of the Prophets, the Son of God.

Your affectionate daughter,

Adina.

LETTER XXVII.

My Dear Father:

Your letter has filled me with joy that I can poorly express by my pen. It assures me that you are certain to leave at the new moon, and after a few days' delay at Gaza, that you will be with me not many days afterward. This letter I shall send to meet you at Gaza.

In it I shall make known to you the particulars of the greatest miracle of power and love above all those wonders which Jesus has done.

When Mary and Martha had despatched the message to Jesus, as I have already stated, they began to be more cheerful with new-born hope, saying:

"If our dear Rabbi, the holy Prophet, comes, he will heal him with a word, as he has done so many of the sick."

"Yes, many whom he knew not he has restored to health by a touch," remarked Martha, "how much more Lazarus, whom he loves as a brother! Oh, that the messenger may press forward with all haste!"

"If Lazarus should die ere he come," hesitatingly remarked my gentle cousin, the wife of John the disciple, "he could bring him to life again, even as he did the Son of the widow of Nain."

"Yes, without doubt, unless it were too late," remarked Martha, shrinking at the thought that her brother should die; "but if he be long dead it will be impossible."

"Nothing is impossible with Jesus," answered Mary, her eyes brightening with trusting faith.

Thus the hours passed between mingled hopes and fears; but ere Jesus came, lo! the mantle of death was laid over the face of their dead brother. "Lazarus is dead, and Jesus is far away!" was the bitter and touching cry made by the bereaved sisters, as they wept in each other's arms.

The next day the burial took place, and yet no messenger came from Jesus. The morning of the third day the man returned, and said that he had found the Prophet on the farther bank of Jordan, where John had baptized, abiding in a humble cottage in the suburbs of Bethabara with his disciples.

The bearer of the sad tidings from the two sisters delivered his simple and touching message:

"Lord, behold he whom thou lovest is sick!"

"And what said he—how did his countenance appear?" asked Martha of the man.

"He betrayed no surprise, but said calmly to me, 'Son, I know it! This sickness shall not be unto death. It shall be for the glory of God; for hereby will my Father permit me to be glorified, that men may see and believe truly that I came out from God.'"

"Alas! He knew not how ill his friend was," said Mary, "or he would not have said it was not unto death, and would surely have hastened with you."

"He has forgotten us," answered Martha. "He should be here to console us in our deep affliction, though he came not to heal our brother."

"Nay, sister, do not think hardly of the blessed friend of Lazarus," said Mary, with soothing tones, as she caressed her elder sister. "I feel that if he had seen fit he could have raised up our brother, even speaking the word from Bethabara. It was not needful he should see him to heal him, for dost thou remember how he healed Lucius, the centurion's son? Yet at the time he was a day's journey distant from him."

"Then why, oh, why, did he not save Lazarus?" exclaimed Martha bitterly.

"In that he did not, sweet sister," answered Mary gently, "it was for the best. Did he not say to the messenger his sickness should be to the glory of his power?"

"But not his death, Mary, not his death! He is dead four days already, and how can the grave give glory to the power of Jesus? Will he raise him up, since corruption hath begun, nay, begun ere we laid him in the cold sepulchre? Oh, speak not to me of the Prophet! He loved not Lazarus, or he had not the power to save him! Nay, leave me, Mary, to the bitterness of my grief."

"Ah, dear Martha, how soon is thy faith in Jesus, when tried, become naught!" said Mary, bending upon her, from her dark, earnest eyes, looks of sad reproach. "Shall one day overturn your years of holy friendship for him? Because he answered not our prayer to come to Lazarus, think you he loved him not, and is indifferent to our anguish? He is wronged by your reproof, and injured by your want of confidence in his love and care for us."

While they were thus discoursing, one came running swiftly towards the house, and breathless with haste, cried to them and to the Jews sitting there, who had come to comfort them concerning their brother:

"The Prophet! The Nazarene! He comes!"

Almost at the same moment Elec, the Gibeonite, entered and said:

"Jesus, Messias of God, is at hand! He already entereth the village followed by his disciples."

At this intelligence the mourners who sat with Mary and Martha in the vine porch, rose up to go and meet him; but Martha, shrieking with the reaction of sudden joy, sprang up and, more quickly than they, reached the street, and flying with great speed, came where Jesus was.

Mary, who had received the news without betraying any other emotion than the secret and holy joy of a heart that had confidence all along in her Lord, instead of hastening to meet him rending her hair with grief, like her sister, proceeded to prepare a room for the hospitable entertainment of the beloved Prophet, when he should come in, thus taking Martha's usual place; and when she had arranged all, she sat down with me in the house, her heart filled with joy and her face expressive of calm and quiet happiness.

When Martha had come near Jesus, whom she met just entering Bethany, walking with four of his disciples along the dusty road, and looking weary and travel-worn, she ran and threw herself at his feet, crying:

"Lord, if thou hadst been here, my brother had not died!"

Jesus taking her hand raised her up, and said with emotion, for he seemed deeply moved by her grief:

"Death to those whom my Father loveth is sleep. The good die not! Lazarus is not dead, but sleepeth, and he shall rise again!"

"I know, O Rabboni, that he shall rise again in the resurrection at the last day."

Jesus then said to her, lifting his celestial glances towards heaven:

"I am the resurrection and the life. He that believeth in me, though he were dead, yet shall he live; and whosoever liveth and believeth in me shall never die! Believest thou this, daughter?"

"Yea, Lord, I believe that thou art the Christ, the Son of God, which should come into the world. I know that whatsoever thou wilt ask of God, God will give it thee, and that even now thou couldst bring Lazarus back again!"

"Corruption and the worm have begun their work," said a proud and unbelieving Pharisee near, on hearing this. "Whatever may have been the state of the ruler's daughter, and of the son of her of Nain, Lazarus the scribe, at least, is dead!"

To this speech Jesus made no reply, but turning to Martha, said softly:

"This day my Father shall be glorified, and the world shall truly know that I am come from Him who is life and the giver of life. Go thou, and tell thy sister that I am here, and would have her come and speak with me."

Martha, then, overjoyed and wondering that Jesus should have known her thoughts, so as to reproach her for her little faith as he had done, hastened to her sister, and entering, cried:

"I have seen the Lord! He calleth for thee, Mary. Come and see him as he sits by Isaiah's fountain, near the market-place."

Mary rose quickly and went out. Certain of her Jewish friends from Jerusalem at that moment met her at the door, and began to comfort her, and to ask her if they also should go with her to weep at the grave of Lazarus, for they said one to another:

"She goes unto the grave to weep there!"

"She goes to see Jesus, the friend of Lazarus, for he calleth her," answered Martha, smiling with eagerness, and speaking with an animation that presented a singular contrast to her late deep grief.

Mary hastened to where Jesus sat by the fountain bathing his dusty and wounded feet.

"Lord," she said, in her sister's words, and with deep emotion, "if thou, Lord, hadst been here, my brother had not died!"

Then bowing her head to the edge of the marble basin, she wept very heavily. The Jews, men and women, who stood about, being touched with her sorrow, also wept, while glittering tears coursed their way down the face of the beloved John, his disciple, who stood near.

Jesus sighed deeply and groaned in spirit as he beheld her grief and their mourning with her. His sacred countenance was marred with the anguish of his soul.

"Rise, let us go to the grave where he lieth," he said to them. "Where have ye laid him?"

"Come, dear Lord, and see," answered Mary, holding him reverently by the sleeve of the robe, and gently yet eagerly drawing him towards the place of the tombs in the vale of Olivet.

In the meanwhile, at home, Martha had been diligently, and with strange cheerfulness, getting in readiness the room of Lazarus. She swept and dusted it, and garnished it with fresh flowers, which she gathered in the little garden.

"This is the rose he set out and loved. This is the violet which blooms immortal. I will place it upon his pillow," she said, with a joyous hilarity softened by the most lovely look of peace, while hope shone in her eyes like twin morning stars ushering in a glorious day. She spoke scarcely above her breath and moved on tiptoe.

"For whom is this preparation, dearest Martha? For Jesus?" I asked.

"Oh, no. The holy Prophet's own room is ready. Mary has prepared that. This is Lazarus' room, and I am decorating it for him."

"Dost thou truly believe that he is coming back from the dead?" I asked, between doubt and strange fear.

"Believe? Oh, yes! I know that nothing is impossible with Jesus! I doubt no more! My faith trembles no longer! He will raise up my brother, and this day he shall sit down at our table with us again, and this night rest his head in peaceful slumber upon this pillow which I am strewing with his favorite flowers. Never had house two such guests as we shall have this day—the Messias of God, and one come back alive from the dead!"

At this moment we heard the noise of the multitude passing by, and it being told us that Jesus was going to the grave, Martha, embracing me with a heavenly smile, drew me gently after her to follow the blessed Prophet to the tomb. All Bethany was in his footsteps.

How shall I describe Jesus as he then appeared? He wore a blue robe, woven without seam throughout, the affectionate work and gift of the two sisters. His face was very pale and sad, yet a certain divine majesty rested thereon, so that his calm, high forehead looked as if it were a throne. His holy, earnest eyes were full of sorrow. His mouth, compressed, betrayed the effort he made to suppress the outbursting of his heart's deep grief.

Slowly he moved onward and, entering the cemetery, he soon stood before the tomb of his beloved friend.

For a few moments he stood gazing upon the closed stone door of the cave in silence. There reigned an expectant hush among the vast throng. Mary knelt at his feet, gazing up into his countenance with a sublime expression of hope and trust. Martha drew softly near and fell upon her knees by the side of her sister. Jesus looked tenderly upon them and, resting his eyes upon the tomb, wept. Large, glittering tears rolled down his cheeks and glanced from his flowing beard to the ground. I knelt by the side of the sisters.

"Behold how he loved him!" whispered the Jews present with surprise.

Others said, "Could not this man which opened the eyes of the blind, have caused that even this man should not have died?"

Jesus, heaving a deep sigh, now came nearer the grave. With a slight movement of his right hand to those who stood by, he said in a tone that, though low, was heard by the whole people, so solemn was the surrounding stillness:

"Take ye away the stone!"

"Lord," said Martha, "by this time the body is offensive, for he hath been dead four days."

"Daughter," said Jesus, looking on her, "believe, and thou shalt behold the power of God."

The men then with some difficulty took away the stone from the door of the sepulchre and stood upon one side. The dark vault yawned with gloomy horrors, and, so corrupt was the air that rushed out, all fell back from it, save Jesus and Mary, retiring several steps from the entrance.

Jesus stood looking into the cave where, as our eyes became accustomed to the darkness within, we could discern the corpse of Lazarus, covered with the grave mantle, and his face bound with a napkin which was already discolored with the sepulchral damp of the grave.

Raising his hands towards heaven and lifting up his spiritual eyes, which were yet moist with tears, Jesus spoke in a voice of indescribable pathos and earnestness of appeal, and with a manner of the most awful reverence, as follows:

"Father, I thank thee that thou hast heard me. And I know that thou hearest me always, but because of the people which stand by do I offer unto thee this prayer, that they may believe that the power I have cometh from thee, and that they may believe that thou hast sent me. And now, O holy Father, may I glorify thee on the earth with the power which thou hast given me."

He then turned towards the tomb, and stretching forth his hand, he cried with a loud voice that made every heart quake:

"Lazarus, come forth!"

My blood stood still in my veins. Scarcely daring to behold, I looked and beheld what all eyes also saw, the corpse rise and stand up within the vault, turn round with its face towards us, and come forth, wrapped hand and foot with the grave-clothes, and his face bound about with a napkin. His countenance was like marble for whiteness, and his eyes, which were open, beamed supernaturally brilliant.

At beholding him a simultaneous shriek burst from the lips of the people, and there was a terrified backward rush of all who were nighest the cave.

Martha, wildly uttering her brother's name, fell forward upon her face insensible.

"Loose him and let him go free!" said Jesus calmly, addressing the petrified and amazed men who had taken away the stone.

Mary was the first one who had the firmness to approach him, and as she began removing the napkin from the sides of his face, others, taking courage by her example, hastened to unswathe his arms and feet. In a few moments he was free from his outer grave-clothes, and the healthful color of his cheeks coming to him, his lips flushed brilliantly with red, his eyes looked natural, beaming with wonder and love as he gazed about him. Perceiving Jesus, he was about to cast himself at his feet in gratitude (for he seemed to have consciousness of all that had happened), but the mighty Prophet drew him to his embrace and kissed him.

But my pen refuses to find language to express the unspeakable emotions of joy and gratitude, words of love and praise, that filled all hearts. Now the great Prophet, now Lazarus, and now Jesus again received the plaudits of the vast throng of people. Hymns were chanted to Jehovah as we passed through the streets, and so many fell down to worship Jesus that it was long before we crossed the threshold of the dwelling, which Jesus did indeed enter with Lazarus by his side! And Martha did see her brother sit at the table, and that night his head rested in deep slumber upon the flower-strewn pillow which her faith and love had prepared for him.

With the hope of soon embracing you, I remain as ever,

Your loving daughter,

Adina.

LETTER XXVIII.

My Dear Father:

Like all my letters, the theme of this will be Jesus, whose claims to be the Messiah I unspeakably rejoice to hear you are beginning to regard with more favorable eyes.

Now Jesus, whose power to work miracles you yourself, my dear father, have confessed must be conferred by Jehovah alone, asserts distinctly and everywhere that he is Messias, the Son of God, the Shiloh of Israel, of whom Moses and the prophets so eloquently wrote. Besides claiming for himself this high character, he was heard, by both my Uncle Amos and myself, in the synagogue at Bethany, two days after he raised Lazarus from the dead, to read from Esaias the words following, and apply them to himself, which he had done before at Nazareth:

"The spirit of the Lord is upon me, because he hath anointed me to preach the gospel to the poor. He hath sent me to heal the broken-hearted, to preach deliverance to the captives, and recovering of sight to the blind; to set at liberty them that are bruised; to preach the acceptable year of the Lord."

The synagogue was thronged, so that people trod upon one another. All eyes were now intent, and all ears were ready to hear what he should speak. He then said unto them:

"This day is this Scripture fulfilled in your ears. Ye ask me, O scribes and men of Israel, to tell you plainly who I am—whether I am the Christ or no. What saith the prophet of Messias when he shall come? Ye have just heard his words. If such works as he prophesieth do show forth themselves in me, know ye not who I am?"

Here a voice cried out in the assembly:

"Tell us plainly, art thou the Christ, the Son of the Highest?"

At this direct inquiry there was intense interest shown to hear the reply.

Jesus seemed about to answer, when a man, who stood near the reading desk, in whom was an unclean spirit, cried out, with a shrieking voice of mingled terror and awe:

"Let me alone! Leave me as I am, thou Jesus of Nazareth! Art thou come hither to destroy me? I know thee who thou art, the Holy One of God!"

Jesus rebuked the devil which possessed the man and said, in the voice of a master commanding a bond slave:

"Hold thy peace, Satan! The Son of man needeth not, though thou givest it, thy testimony. Hold thy peace, and come out of the man!"

At this word the man uttered a fearful cry of despair and rage, and foaming at the mouth cast himself, or rather was thrown down by the devil within him, to the ground; where, after a moment's terrific struggle, with contortions of bodily anguish, he lay senseless as if dead. Jesus took him by the hand, and he stood up and, looking in the face of the Prophet with earnestness and wonder, burst into tears of gratitude, exclaiming:

"I am escaped as a bird out of the snare of the fowler; the snare is broken, and I am escaped. God hath delivered me out of the hand of my enemy!" He then sat at the feet of Jesus, calm, grateful, happy, and in his right mind! All gazed on him with wonder, while from the great mass of the people rose a great shout, for they were all amazed, saying:

"This is none other than the Christ, the Son of David! This is the King of Israel!" while the loud shouts of "Hosanna! hosanna! hosanna!" cheered by a thousand voices, "Hosanna to our King!" shook like a passing storm the synagogue.

When the noise had a little subsided, some of the Scribes and Pharisees said, reproving him for not rebuking these cries:

"Who is this that suffereth himself to be hailed as king? This is treason to the emperor!"

Jesus then said in a loud, clear voice:

"My kingdom is not of this world! I seek not an earthly throne or earthly sceptre. My kingdom is from above. Ye say truly, I am king," he added, with indescribable majesty, "and hereafter ye shall behold me sitting upon the throne of heaven."

When he had thus far spoken he could not proceed farther, on account of the sudden and immense uproar which his words produced. Some shouted, "Hosanna!" others said he blasphemed; one cried for the Roman guard, another for the priests, to eject him from the tribune; many rushed towards him to cast themselves at his feet, while many, putting their fingers in their ears, hurried forth from the synagogue, crying:

"His blasphemies will cause the house to fall upon us and crush us!"

Never was such an uproar heard. In the midst of it Jesus conveyed himself away, none knew whither; and when I returned to the house of Martha I heard his low, earnest, touching voice in prayer to God in his little chamber. He had sought its sacred quiet to be alone with his Father in heaven. At times I could hear him praying and supplicating, in tones of the most heart-breaking pathos; at others the silence of his room was only broken at intervals by sighs and pitiful groans that seemed to come from a breaking and crushed heart. Oh, what hand may remove the veil and reveal what passed there in that holy retirement between the Prophet and his God!

It was late in the day when he came forth, Martha having softly tapped at his door to say that the evening meal was prepared and alone waited for him. When he appeared his face was colorless and bore traces of weeping, and though he smiled kindly upon us all, as he was wont to do, there was a deep-seated sorrow upon his countenance that brought tears to my eyes. Æmilius joined us at the table, and with dear Lazarus and with Uncle Amos, we passed a sacred hour; for the Prophet ate not, but talked to us much and sweetly of the love of God, and as all listened the viands were forgotten.

Pardon me, dearest father, if I am too warm and urgent in my efforts to bring you to accept Jesus as the Christ. Convinced, as I am, that he is Messias, I cannot but ardently desire that you, also, should come to the knowledge of this truth. What he is yet to be, how he is yet to develop his majesty and power, is unknown to us all. Some do think that he will enter Jerusalem ere long, attended by tens of thousands of his followers, and that before him Pilate will peaceably vacate his Procuratorial chair, and retire, not only from the Holy City but from Judea, with his legions; that Jesus will ascend the throne of David, and the glory of the age of Solomon be revived under his rule.

Such, dear father, is the future of the Prophet, as looked for by all his disciples save one, and this is John, the husband of my Cousin Mary. John, on hearing our views of the coming glory of the Prophet, looks compassionate and says:

"His kingdom is not of this world. He has naught to do with the splendors of earth. His glory you will behold, but it is a glory of the spirit. Ere perceiving it fully we may first pass through the valley of darkness, the gate of the tomb. He has distinctly said to me, 'I must first suffer many things at the hands of men before I enter upon my reign of glory. The Jews will seek me to kill me, and I shall be taken from among you; but let not sorrow fill your hearts. Death can have no power over me save such as I permit it to hold. I lay down my life and I take it again. Through much tribulation and sorrow must the Son of God win the sceptre of this earth—the hearts of men. I shall conquer, but to do so I must fall. Yet fear not. My death shall be the gateway to Paradise for you all!'"

Thus, dear father, do we discourse together about this wonderful Prophet, whose future life is all a mystery, save that, from the prophecies, we know it is to be inconceivably glorious; from his own lips, to be inconceivably sorrowful. But whether on a throne, giving laws to the world, or in the dust, borne down by the deepest woe, I shall still love, honor, reverence him and trust in him as my Savior, my Prince, and the Holy One of God!

Your devoted and loving,

Adina.

LETTER XXIX.

My Dearest Father:

With what emotions of grief and amazement I commence this letter you can form no just conception. Jesus, the Prophet of God, is a prisoner to the Roman power!

But I fear not the issue! He cannot be holden of his foes, save by his own free will. He can, with a word, turn his chains into bands of sand, and by a glance render his guards dead men. He will, therefore, escape their bonds. They can have no power over him.

It seems that to-day, after eating the Passover with his twelve chosen friends, and instituting a new and peculiar feast with wine and bread, which he told them impressively would be his last supper with them, he went forth towards Olivet, and there, seating himself beneath the shade of a tree, he talked with them very sadly, saying that "his hour was come, that he had ended his work, and that he was about to be delivered into the hands of sinful men."

John gave the following narrative: "It was evening, and the south side of Olivet lay in deep shadow. We were all sorrowful. We felt, each one of us, as if some grievous evil was pending over us. The tones of our beloved Master's voice moved us to tears, quite as much as his words, which latter were full of mystery. We were all present except Iscariot, who had remained in the city to discharge the costs—he being our purse-bearer—of the Passover supper and pay for the hire of the room. At that supper Jesus had said very plainly that one of our number would betray him into the hands of the priests. At hearing our Lord say these strange words in accents of touching reproach, we were all deeply moved, and Peter and the rest at once questioned him individually, if it were they. 'Lord, is it I?' and another, 'Lord, is it I?' I was resting, at the moment, with my face on the shoulder of Jesus, and said softly, 'Lord, who is it that betrayeth thee? I will forthwith lay hands upon him and prevent his doing thee harm.' Jesus shook his head and smiling gently, said:

"'My beloved brother, thou knowest not what thou would do. The Son of man must needs be betrayed by his own friends, but woe unto him who betrayeth me! Mark which of the twelve dippeth bread with me into the dish!'

"I looked and saw Judas reach forward and dip into the dish at the same instant with Jesus; but in his eagerness, or from conscious guilt, his hand trembled, he spilled the salt over the board, and the sop fell from his grasp into the bowl; upon which Jesus gave him the piece he held, saying to him, with a remarkable expression in his clear, piercing eyes:

"'Judas, that thou doest, do quickly!'

"Instantly Judas rose from the table, and without a reply or casting a look at any of us, went out.

"For a few moments after his footsteps had ceased to be heard, there prevailed a heavy silence in the chamber, for a strange fear had fallen upon us; why, we could not tell; and looking into one another's faces, and then into our dear Master's, we seemed to await some dread event. His face was placid and full of affection as he looked upon us. The momentary cloud which shaded the noble profile when he spoke to Judas had all passed off, and there was the serenity of a cloudless sky in his face."

"What was the mysterious feast which he instituted?" asked Mary, interrupting John here.

"You may properly call it mysterious," he answered. "As we were eating the Passover, Jesus took up bread and, blessing it by a solemn act of consecration, broke it with his hands and gave a portion to each of us, saying with it, 'Take, eat; this is my body!'

"Awed and impressed by his manner and the act, we all received and ate it as he commanded us to do, as reverently as if it were the holy shew-bread of the Temple, dedicated to God's use. When we had eaten in silence what we perceived was the inauguration of a new and most sacred feast by his own hand, he took up the cup of wine, and consecrated it also by giving thanks and blessing. The hallowed cup he now offered to each one of us. We all drank of it with deep devotion, for he said to us, 'I will drink no more with you the fruit of the vine until that day that I drink it new in the kingdom of God!' He also said of the wine, 'This is my blood!'"

"And how do you understand these words, that the bread consecrated was his body, and the wine was his blood?" I asked of the disciple.

"That is an inquiry I cannot answer," said John. "It is a mystery. But the Lord says it shall be made clear to us by and by.

"We then sang the Passover hymn to God, and went out at his command to go to Olivet. As we went he discoursed with us:

"'My children,' he said. 'I am to be with you but a little while longer. The hour of my departure is at hand. Remember my last words—love one another. In this shall all men know that ye are my disciples.'

"'Lord,' cried Peter, 'we will go with thee! Thou shalt not leave us nor go without us!'

"Thus we all, eagerly and tearfully, gathered around him, alarmed and grieved at the words he had said. He regarded us lovingly and said:

"'Little children, I must leave you. Whither I go you cannot come!'

"'Though thou wentest to the uttermost parts of the sea, I will follow thee, my Master and Lord!' exclaimed Peter. 'Whither goest thou, that we may not follow? I will lay down my life for thee; and so will all these!'

AN ORIENTAL SUPPER SCENE.

"'Wilt thou die for me, Peter?' asked Jesus, gazing on him with a sad, sweet look. 'Verily, verily, Peter, thou little knowest thyself. The cock shall not crow twice ere thou shalt thrice deny that thou knowest me.'

"'Deny thee, Lord!' repeated Peter, with amazed grief and horror in his looks.

"'Yes, Peter,' answered Jesus, firmly but kindly, 'deny that thou ever knewest me; for the time draweth near when there shall be safety only in confessing ignorance of Jesus the Nazarene. And all ye,' he added, while his voice grew tremulous, and tears glistened in his eyes, 'all ye shall be offended because of me this night; ye shall be ashamed that ye are my disciples, and ye will think me a deceiver and will be displeased at me. Yea, every one of you shall desert me; for thus it is written: "The shepherd shall be smitten, and the sheep shall be scattered!"'

"When he saw that our hearts were troubled and that we were sad, and that the faithful Philip sobbed aloud at being supposed capable of abandoning his Master, he added, 'Let not your hearts be troubled; I go to prepare a place for you in my Father's house!'

"'Thy father, Lord, no longer liveth in Nazareth; and, were he alive, there are but two small apartments in his humble house,' said Thomas. 'How sayest thou that we are all to lodge there?'

"'Thomas, thou canst understand only what thine eyes see. I speak of my Father who is in heaven. In his house are many mansions.'

"Jesus then, as we drew near Cedron, began plainly to tell us that he was to die, and that by his death we should be admitted into a heavenly paradise and live forever. We could not understand all he said, but we knew that he was soon to be taken from us and sorrow filled all our hearts. After discoursing with us in the most touching words, he at length said:

"'Come, let us go over Cedron to the side of Olivet, into the garden we so much love to walk in.'

"We went with him, inclosing him as a guard, to conceal his person from the Jewish spies, as well as to defend him. Peter and James went before. The full moon shone brightly, and by its light glancing on the face of Jesus, by whom I walked, I saw that it was sadder than its wont, while he spoke but little.

"We at length crossed the brook and entered the dark groves of Olivet. Familiar with all the paths, we advanced to a central group of venerable olive trees, beneath which, tradition says, Abraham used to sit; and there Jesus, turning to us, said in a voice of the deepest woe:

"'Friends, the hour of my time of trial is come! My work is ended. I would be alone. Remain you here and watch, for we shall be sought for. Come with me, Peter, and you also, James. I am going to pray yonder.'

"'Take me, also, dear Lord!' I said, sorrowfully.

"'Yes, thou art always with me, beloved!' he answered. 'I will not leave thee now.'

"So leaving the eight friends to keep watch against the intrusion of his enemies, who were known to be everywhere seeking him, he walked away to the most secluded recesses of the garden. He stopped at the place near the rock where Adam is said to have hidden from Jehovah, and saying to us in a sorrowful tone, 'Tarry ye here, while I go apart and pray to my Father,' he went from us about a stone's cast and kneeled down, where a thick olive branch hanging low to the ground concealed him from our view. I was so solicitous lest he should leave us and we should see him no more, that I soon softly advanced near to the spot and beheld him prostrate on the ground, while deep groans broke from his heart. I heard his voice murmuring, but could not distinguish the words broken by grief; only the tones were those of strange horror and dread.

"As he prayed thus in great agony, I suddenly beheld a swift light pass by me, as if from the skies, and lo! an angel stood by the side of Jesus, bending over him and raising him up from the ground. A soft, bright glory shone around the spot, so that Peter, seeing it, advanced towards me, supposing some one had entered the garden bearing a torch. I beckoned to Peter to be motionless, and he gazed with me in speechless astonishment and admiration upon the form of the angel, from whose glorious face was emitted the radiance which illumined the place where Jesus was. As the angel raised Jesus from the ground, we saw that his divine countenance was convulsed with anguish, and upon his brow stood great shining drops of sweat, mingled with blood, which oozed from his pallid temples and, rolling down his marble cheeks, dropped to the ground. Never had we beheld a human visage so marred by sorrow, so deeply graven with the lines of agony.

"The angel seemed to utter soothing words, and pointed with his shining hand towards heaven, as if to encourage him with hope and give him strength. The face of Jesus grew more serene; he raised his eyes heavenward with a divine expression of holy love, and cried in a strong voice:

"'Thy will, not mine, O God, be done!'

"The angel then embraced him, as if strengthening him, and soaring upward, disappeared like a star returning into the blue depths of heaven, while Peter and I stood by wondering and full of awe at what we beheld.

"We remained for some time conversing together upon the wonderful vision we had seen, which confirmed us in the certainty that Jesus came from God, and was in truth the Messias that should come; but at length, wearied with our day's excitements, we must have fallen asleep, for we were suddenly startled by the voice of our dear Master saying:

"'Why sleep ye, children? But the hour is past for watching. Ye may sleep on now, for though your flesh is weary, your spirit is willing. I need your aid no longer!'

"While he was speaking, we saw many torches gleaming through the trees, along King David's walk, and the tramp of feet fell on our ears. We soon saw a large party advancing into the midst of the garden, who walked rapidly and spoke only in undertones. We at once took the alarm and said to Jesus:

"'Fly, dear Master! Let us ascend the hill, and escape by the way of Bethany, for these are enemies!'

"'Nay,' answered our dear Master. 'It must needs be that I deliver myself into the hands of these men. How else shall the Scriptures be fulfilled? Seek safety in flight for yourselves, but I must go whither they will lead me.'

"'Not so, Lord,' answered Peter. 'There is time for thee to escape; or, if not, we will stand by thee and defend thee.'

"So said all the disciples. Jesus shook his head and said, with a sad smile, 'Ye know not what ye say or would do. Mine hour is come!'

"While he yet spake the multitude drew nearer, and those who had the lead, raising their torches high above their heads, discovered us, with Jesus in the midst. To my surprise I beheld Judas acting as their guide, for he alone knew where his Master was to be found at that hour. Upon discovering Jesus this wicked man ran forward, with expressions of friendship in his face, and kissed Jesus on the cheek, saying:

"'Hail, Master! I am glad I have found thee!'

"'Judas,' said Jesus, 'betrayest thou the Son of man with a kiss?'

"When Judas heard this he turned to the multitude, at the head of which I recognized some of the chief priests, and of the most learned scribes of the Temple, and cried aloud:

"'This is he! Seize him, and hold him fast!'

"Thereupon the crowd, to the number of full ten score men, among whom were the vilest sort of people, rushed forward to lay hands upon Jesus, the moon and torches together shedding almost the bright light of day into the garden upon the whole group.

MOUNT OF OLIVES.

"At seeing them advance so furiously, with spears and clubs and swords, Peter and James placed themselves before Jesus to defend him, while I, being unarmed, cast myself across his breast, to shield his heart with my body. The more bold men in the crowd coming too near, Peter smote one of them with his sword, as he was reaching out his arm to grasp Jesus by the shoulder, and clave off his ear. At seeing this the crowd uttered a fierce shout, and were pressing upon us, when Jesus raised the palm of his hand and said quietly:

"'Whom seek ye?'

"Instantly the whole mass rolled backward, like a receding billow rebounding from the face of an immovable rock, and every man thereof fell with his forehead to the ground, where they all lay for a minute stunned. We twelve alone stood, for Judas had not been struck down, and now remained gazing with amazement and terror upon the prostrate enemies of Jesus.

"'Lord,' cried Peter, astonished, 'if thou canst thus repel thy foes, thou needest not fear them more. Shall I smite Judas also?'

"'Nay, put up thy sword, Peter! Let him remain to witness my power, that he may know that he nor his have any power over me save that I give them.'

"While he was thus speaking the people and soldiers rose to their feet, and, instead of flying, they seemed to be infuriated at their discomfiture; and the chief priests crying out that it was by sorcery that they had been thus stricken down, they rushed madly forward and laid their hands upon Jesus and upon us all. In vain I contended against numbers to rescue Jesus; overpowered, we were defeated and driven from the garden, leaving Jesus in the hands of his enemies."

When John had gone thus far in his relation, dear father, our tears and his were mingled. But we try and comfort ourselves with the word of his promise:

"Ye know not now, but ye shall know by and by, and shall believe truly that I came out from God. What now seems to you mysterious shall be made clear as light. Wait and have faith, and all shall be made known which now you understand not. Let no trials and degradations ye see me pass through cause your faith to fail. I am come into this world to conquer; but if I stoop, it is to raise up the world with me when I rise again!"

I have omitted to mention to you what more John related as wonderful touching the arrest of the Prophet. "As the chief priests bound and laid their hands on him, there was," he said, "heard in the air the sound of myriads of rushing wings, and notes like the gathering signal of a trumpet, echoing and re-echoing in the skies, as if a countless host of invisible beings were marshaling, armies by armies, in mid-heaven! At these fearful and sublime sounds all raised their heads but could behold nothing. Then Jesus said, with a majestic and commanding look, such as I had never before beheld upon his face:

"'Ye hear that I am not without heavenly friends! I have only to pray to my Father which is in heaven, and he will bid twelve legions of his angels, now hovering in the air and yearning to defend me from my foes, descend to my aid! But I desire not to use my powers for myself.'"

Thus, dear father, was Jesus borne away by a fierce multitude and dragged into the city.

John, whose interest in and affection for Jesus led him to follow them, heard all this; but Jesus made no answer, only walking quietly along, patiently enduring all they said and did.

As they entered the city gate the Roman guard, seeing the immense crowd and uproar, stopped them to learn the cause of the commotion.

"'We have here a traitor and conspirator, O captain of the guard,' answered Eli, the chief priest: 'a pestilent fellow, who calls himself Christ, a king! We have, therefore, with this band of hired soldiers, taken him, as he was met secretly with twelve of his fellow-conspirators, plotting to overthrow the government of Cæsar and make himself king of Judea.'

"'Long live Cæsar! Long live the emperor!' shouted the Roman soldiers. 'We have no king but Augustus Imperator!'

"Upon this many of the soldiers cried, 'Take him before the Procurator! He will give him his deserts, who would take his procuratorship away from him! To Pilate! To Pilate!'

"'To Annas!' shouted the Jews. 'First to Annas!'

"Then, with some shouting one thing and others another thing, he was hurried towards the house of Annas.

"When Annas knew that the prisoner was Jesus, he uttered a fearful oath expressive of his joy and wicked satisfaction, and, hastily robing and coming down into the court, he bade them bring the prisoner in. But the calm majesty of Jesus abashed him, and checked the course of insulting questions he began putting to him. At length finding that the Prophet would make no reply, he caused him to be bound still more closely with more cords, lest he should, like Samson, rend his bonds and escape on the way, and sent him to Caiaphas, the High Priest, saying to him:

"'Caiaphas will find voice for thy tongue, O Prophet! So, thou wouldst destroy the Temple, and callest thyself the Son of the Lord Jehovah! Out, blasphemer! Away with him, or the house will be swallowed up with the presence of one so impious! Away with the man! By the crown of David! Pilate will make thee king in truth, and give thee a Roman throne, to which, so that thou mayest not presently fall from it, he will nail thee foot and hand!'

"At this the cruel crowd shouted their approbation, and many cried:

"'Ay, to the cross! to the cross with him!'

"But others said, 'Nay, but to Caiaphas!'

"The captain of the Roman soldiers resolved that he should be taken before Pilate, and led the way thither, Jesus bound in the midst."

With renewed uproar they tumultuously pressed forward, their way lighted by the red glare of a hundred torches, insulting the Roman soldiers with seditious cries. John followed, but being recognized as one of his disciples by a soldier in Æmilius' legion, he was seized and only escaped by leaving his apparel in the grasp of the rude Roman. Five of the disciples who have escaped arrest, are now in this house, whither John fled also, on eluding the grasp of the soldier, leaving his linen garment in his hand. We are all so sad and anxious! To move in favor of Jesus is only to share his fate and do him no service.

Yet through all, dear father, I do trust in him and hope! Oh, I cannot doubt his truth and power! I have seen him bring Lazarus up from the grave, and I will not believe but that he can save himself, and will save himself, from their hands. It is only when I shall behold him really no more—see him really dead—that my faith in his divine mission will waver.

With eyes blinded with tears, I can scarcely subscribe myself,

Your sad but loving daughter,

Adina.

LETTER XXX.

My Dear Father:

I know not how to write—I know not what to say! Dismay and sorrow fill my heart! I feel as if life were a burden too heavy to bear! They have crucified him!

Verily fear and a snare are come upon us—desolation and destruction, O my father! We know not which way to turn. He in whom we trusted has proved as one of us, weak and impotent, and has suffered death without power to save himself. He that saved others could not escape the death of the Roman cross! While I write, I hear the priest Abner, in the court below, mocking my Uncle Amos in a loud voice:

"Your Messias is dead! A famous great prophet, surely, you Nazarenes have chosen—born in a manger and crucified as a thief! Said I not that he who could speak against the Temple and the priesthood was of Beelzebub?"

Rabbi Amos makes no reply. Shame and despair seal his lips. Thus our enemies triumph over us, and we answer only with confusion of face.

This unexpected, this unlooked-for, startling result has stupefied me, and not only me but all who have been so led by fascination as to trust in him. Even John, the beloved disciple, I hear now pacing the floor of the adjoining room, sobbing as if his noble heart would burst. Mary, my cousin's sweet voice, I catch from time to time trying to soothe him, although she is stricken like us all to the very earth. The unhappy John I hear despairingly answer her:

"Do not try to comfort me, Mary! There is no ground for hope more! He is dead—dead! All is lost! We who trusted in him have only to fly, if we would save our wretched lives, into Galilee, and return once more to our nets! The sun which shone so dazzlingly has proved a phantom light and gone out in darkness! He whom I could not but love, I see that I loved too well, since he proves not what I believed him to be! Oh, how could he be so like the Son of God and yet not be! Yet I loved and adored him as if he were the very Son of the Highest! But I have seen him die as a man—I have gazed on his lifeless body! I have beheld the deep wound made into his very heart by the Roman spear! I cast myself upon him, when he was taken down from the cross, and implored him, by his love for me, to give some sign that he was not holden by death! I placed my trembling hands over his heart. It was still—still—motionless as stone, like any other dead man's! He was dead—dead! With him die all our hopes—the hopes of Israel!"

"He may live again," said Mary, softly and hesitatingly, as if she herself had no such hope. "He raised Lazarus, thou dost remember!"

"Yes, for Jesus was living to do it," answered John, stopping in his walk; "but how can the dead raise the dead? No, he will never move, speak, nor breathe again!"

But I will not further delay the account of his trial and condemnation, for you will be anxious to know how such a man could be condemned to a malefactor's death. In my last letter I spoke of his arrest through the traitorous part enacted by Judas. Led by his captors, bound by the wrists with a cord, Jesus was taken from the dark groves of Olivet, where he had been found at prayer, and conducted with great noise into the city by Cæsar's gate. It is near this archway that Rabbi Amos lives. I will copy for you my Cousin Mary's account of it to Martha of Bethany, just written by her, instead of adding any more to my own.

"I went out upon the basilica, which overlooked the streets," says Mary, "and beheld a multitude advancing with torches flashing, and soon they came opposite the house, at least two hundred men in number, half clad and savage looking, with fierce eyes and scowling looks. Here and there among them was a Levite urging them on, and I also beheld Abner the priest firing their passions by loud oratory and eager gesticulations. Behind rode five Roman horsemen, with levelled spears, guarding a young man who walked with a firm step. I burst into tears. It was Jesus! His locks were dishevelled, his beard torn, his face marred, and his garments rent. He was pale and suffering, yet walked with a firm step. I burst into tears, and so did Adina, who had come out to see what was passing. He looked up and said touchingly, 'Mourn not for me.'

"He would have said more, but the priest smote him rudely upon the mouth, and the crowd, following his example, would have done him further insult but for the Roman soldiers, who turned their spears every way to guard him from violence, for they had rescued him from the terrible rage of the Jews by their centurion's orders, and were commanded to bring him safely before Pilate. So, thus guarded and escorted by the men who thirsted for his blood, he was led onward to the Pretorium, where the Roman Procurator resided. Gradually the whole multitude disappeared in the distance when silence, a dread and unearthly silence, succeeded. I turned and looked in Adina's face. She was leaning, as colorless as marble, against one of the columns of the basilica.

"'What can all this mean?' she said, with emotion. 'Can it be possible he has suffered himself to be taken—he who could destroy or make alive with a word? What means this dreadful scene we have just witnessed?'

"I could not answer. All I knew was what my eyes just beheld—that Jesus our Prophet, our King, our Messias, on whom all our hopes and the joy of Israel rested, was dragged a prisoner through the streets, helpless and without a helper. I trembled with I knew not what unknown forebodings. Suddenly Adina cried:

"'He cannot be harmed! He cannot die! He is a mighty Prophet, and has power that will strike his enemies dead. Let us not fear. He has yielded himself only the more terribly to defeat and destroy his foes. We will not fear what Pilate or the priests will do! They cannot harm the Anointed Shiloh of the Lord!'

"While we were yet talking, dear Martha, a dark figure passed stealthily along beneath the basilica, and seemed to court the shadows of the house. At this moment my father, Rabbi Amos, opened the outer gate, with a torch in his hand, to follow, at our request, the crowd of people, and see what should befall Jesus. The light glared full upon the tall, spare form of Peter, the Galilean fisherman. His dark, stern features wore an expression of earnest anxiety.

"'Is it thou, Peter?' exclaimed my father. 'What is all this? Who has ordered the arrest of Jesus? What has he done?'

"'That hateful and envious man, Caiaphas, seeks to destroy him, and has bribed with large lures of gold the baser Jews to do this thing. Come with me, Rabbi, and let us die with him!' and the Galilean pressed eagerly forward at a pace with which my father could not keep up.

"And this was an hour ago, and yet no news has come from the Pretorium; but from time to time a dreadful shout from the hill on which the palace of Caiaphas stands, breaks upon my ears, and the glare of unseen torches illumines the atmosphere high above the towers of the palace. It is a fearful night of agony and suspense. Adina, in her painful uncertainty, but for my entreaties would go forth alone towards the Pretorium to hear and know all. I can keep myself calm only by writing to you. Adina has also commenced a letter to her father, recording these sad things, but she drops her pen to start to the balcony at every sound. When will this fearful night end! What will the morrow reveal!

"It is an hour since I wrote the last line. The interval has been one of agony. Rumors have reached us that the priests insist on Pilate's passing sentence of death on the Prophet. The cries, 'Crucify him! Crucify him!' have distinctly reached our ears. John is now here. About half an hour after

Jesus passed he reached our house nearly destitute of apparel, his clothing having been torn from off him by the Jews, in their efforts to make him their prisoner also. He is calm and confiding, saying that his beloved Master can never be injured by them, and that he will ere many hours deliver himself from his foes, and proclaim himself king of Israel with power such as man never had before. May the God of Jacob defend him! John has just gone up to the Temple to get news, in disguise of a priest, wearing my father's robes.

"I have just seen a messenger passing in great haste along the street, and his horse falling, cast him almost upon our threshold. It was the page of Æmilius, the noble Roman knight, who is betrothed to my Cousin Adina. She hastened to his aid. He was but stunned, and soon was able to say that he bore a message from Lucia Metella, the fair and youthful bride of Pilate, urging him to have nothing to do with the Prophet, but to give him his liberty, for she had just awakened from an impressive dream in which she saw him sitting on the throne of the universe, crowned with the stars of heaven, the earth a footstool beneath his feet, and all nations assembled and doing him homage.

"This report of the page has filled our hearts with joy and hope inexpressible. Confident that Jesus is the Son of God, we will not fear what man can do unto him.

"My father has returned. It is day. He says nothing can save Jesus but his own divine power. The Jews are in number many thousands, and cry for his blood. Pilate has but a cohort of soldiers and fears to use force, lest the exasperated people break into open revolt and take the city from his hands, which they can with ease do if they will unite. 'He trembles,' said my father, 'between fear to condemn the innocent and dread of the vengeance of the Jews if he let him go. Nothing can save the Prophet but his own mighty miracle-working power. He who has saved others will surely save himself.'

"While my father was speaking a man rushed into our presence. He was low in stature, broad-chested, with a stiff, reddish beard, narrow eyes, and sharp, unpleasant visage. His attire was ragged and mean, as was his whole aspect. He grasped in his right hand a small bag, which rung with coin as his shaking fingers held it. He trembled all over, and seizing my father by the arm with the quick, nervous grasp of a lunatic, cried hoarsely:

"'Will he let them? Will he? Will he?'

"'Will he what, Iscariot? Of whom do you speak? Art thou crazed? Thou shouldst well be, after thy deed to-night!'

"'Will he let them kill him? Will he die? Will he die? Think you he will escape? He can if he will! Cords to him are ropes of sand!'

"'No, no. He is bound hand and foot!' answered my father, sadly. 'He makes no defense. I fear he will let them do as they will with him. He makes no effort to save his life.'

"At this Judas, for it was that wicked man, beat his knitted forehead in a frenzied manner with the bag of silver, and with a look of horrible despair rushed forth, crying as he went:

"'I will save him! The priests shall have their money again! He shall not die! If I had believed he would not do some miracle to escape them, I never would have sold him! I hoped to get their money, and trusted, if they bound him, for him to escape by his own power. I did not dream that he would not exert it to save himself. I will save thee, innocent man of God, for I, not thou, alone am guilty! Oh, if I had suspected this—but he shall not die!'

"With these ravings he disappeared towards the Pretorium, leaving us all amazed at what we had heard.

"The sun is up. The fate of Jesus is sealed! The Procurator has signed the sentence of death and he is to be crucified to-day. But, with Judas, I believe that he cannot die, and that he will signalize the hour by some wonderful miracle of personal deliverance. Thus, tremblingly, we hope and wait."

Here terminates, my dear father, what my cousin has written to Martha and Lazarus.

Your sorrowing but loving daughter,

Adina.

LETTER XXXI.

Dearest Father:

I have only terminated my last letter to take up my pen for the beginning of another, for I find relief only in writing to you from the deep affliction which has struck me to the earth. If anything can add to my mortification at the death of the Nazarene, Jesus, it is that I shall have endeavored so earnestly to make you believe in him also. Oh, I shall never have confidence in a human being again; and the more lovely, the more holy, the more heavenly the character of any one, the wiser and purer their teachings, the more distrustful shall I be of them.

But I will turn from these painful thoughts and, as I promised in my last, will give you an account of what passed at his trial.

It is now the morning following the crucifixion, and I am calmer than I was yesterday and will be able to write with more coherency. Twenty-four hours have passed since he was nailed to the cross. His followers have been, since his arrest, hunted like wild beasts of the wilderness. Annas has hired and filled with wine fierce Roman soldiers, and sent them everywhere to seize the fugitive Nazarenes. John was especially sought out, and the emissaries of Annas came at midnight last night to the house to take him, but we assisted him in making his escape by means of the subterranean passage that leads from the dwelling of Rabbi Amos to the catacombs beneath the Temple.

Æmilius, though only recently a convert from the paganism of Rome, is firm in his faith that Jesus will rise again to life; and, instead of giving up all, as we do, he says that he should not be amazed to be suddenly told by the soldiers, whom he left to guard his tomb, that he had burst forth alive from the dead!

But I have forgotten that I am to narrate to you, dear father, the particulars of his accusation, trial and condemnation. As I was not present in the Pretorium, I am indebted for the further details which I shall give, in part to John and in part to Rabbi Amos.

"As soon as the mob of Jews who had Jesus under arrest, and which I saw pass the house, reached the abode of Rabbi Annas, he asked them whom they had in custody, and when they answered that it was the great Nazarene Prophet, he said with joy:

"'Bring him into the lower court, that I may see him. By the rod of Aaron, I would have him do some notable miracle for me.'

"And thus speaking, the white-headed old man hastened down to the court, which, on reaching, he found thronged with the infuriated multitude. It was with difficulty he made a passage to where Jesus stood, both imprisoned and defended by a glittering lattice of Roman spears. After regarding him attentively he said, with curiosity yet with sarcasm:

"'Art thou, then, the King of the Jews? Hast thou come to reign on the throne of David? Show me a sign from heaven, and I will acknowledge thee, O Nazarene!'

"But Jesus stood calm and dignified, making no answer. Annas then angrily plucked him by the beard, and a messenger at the same moment arrived to say to him that Caiaphas, the High Priest, demanded to have Jesus brought before him. Upon this he said in a loud voice:

"'Lead him to the palace! Caiaphas, my son-in-law, would see the man who would destroy the Temple and rebuild it in three days!'

"There now arose a dreadful shout from the priests and people, who, rushing upon Jesus, cried, 'Crucify him!' and attempted to grasp his person, as they guarded him along the streets; but in protecting him, as they had been commanded to do, the Romans wounded several of the Jews. Hereupon there was a great cry of sedition and shouts of:

"'Down with the Roman eagles! Down with the barbarians! Death to the Gentiles!'

"These cries were followed up by a fearful rush of the mass of men upon the handful of guards. They were forced back, their spears broken like straws or turned aside, and Jesus successfully wrested from their power. But in the height of the battle Æmilius appeared with a portion of the legion of which he was Prefect, and instantly charging the people, who fled before the breasts of his horses, rescued the Prophet.

"'Rabbi,' said Æmilius to the Prophet, with compassionate respect, 'I know thou hast power from God to disperse as chaff this rabble of fiends. Speak, and let them perish at thy divine command!'

"'Nay, my son. I am come into the world for this hour,' answered Jesus. 'This, also, is a part of my mission from my Father. It becomes me to endure all things, even death.'

"'You cannot die, my Lord,' said Æmilius warmly. 'Did I not see thee raise Lazarus from the tomb?'

"'To die I came into this world, but not for myself. I lay down my life, and I can take it again. These men could have no power over me except my Father did grant it to them. And what my Father willeth I will also. Seek not, my son, to deliver me.'

"These words passed between them beneath the portico, as Æmilius was loosing the sharp cords from the bleeding wrists of the youthful Prophet.

"'To Caiaphas! To Caiaphas!' now cried the multitude, who had been for a moment awed by the bold charge of the Roman horse, but now grew bolder as some men removed the dead and wounded out of sight. 'To the palace with the blasphemer! for he who calls himself God is, by our law, to be punished with death! To the High Priest with him!'

"'I can rescue you, great Prophet!' said Æmilius resolutely. 'Give me the word, and you are mounted on my horse and safe in the castle of David.'

"'The High Priest has sent for me. He must be obeyed,' answered Jesus; and Æmilius, surprised at his refusal to escape, reluctantly escorted him to the palace. The windows already glared with torches, and the superb Hall of Aaron was alight with a hundred flambeaux. Caiaphas was already upon his throne, although it was long past the hour of midnight—an unwonted time for him to sit in the council chamber; but his desire to have Jesus brought before him led him to hold an extraordinary court. A score of the elders and chief priests were standing about him, their dark, eager faces earnestly watching the entrance to get a look at the approaching Prophet. As Jesus serenely entered, led by the sorrowful Æmilius, Caiaphas bent his tall, gaunt form forward, thrust his neck and huge head in advance, and with keen eyes and sharp, scrutinizing glances, surveyed him whom he jealously looked upon as his foe.

"The multitude, pressing in, soon filled the vast hall and even crowded upon the rostrum, upon which were seated the scribes, elders and many of the principal priests. The Roman soldiers, with clanging steel, marched in, and arrayed themselves on either side of the High Priest's throne, leaving Jesus standing alone before its footstool.

"Contrasting with the brilliancy of the gorgeous hall and the glittering robes of the priests, surged and heaved and moved below the dark masses of the people, in their gray and brown caps and cloaks, for the night was cold and they wore their winter garments; and all this wild ocean of human forms gleamed with ten thousand eyes, flashing like the phosphorescent stars that glitter on the surface of the upheaving sea when the shadow of the storm-cloud hangs above it, and the winds are about to be unbound to lash it into fury. So seemed this terrible sea of human heads—Jesus the center of their looks and of their hate. He alone, of all that countless host, he alone was calm, serene, fearless! Caiaphas now waved his hand, with a gesture for silence, and addressed Jesus:

"'So, then,' he spoke, with haughty irony, 'thou art Jesus, the far-famed Galilean prophet! Men say thou canst raise the dead! We would fain behold a miracle. Thinkest thou, if we put thee to death presently, thou canst raise thyself?'

"'Jesus,' saith Rabbi Amos, who stood near him and saw all, 'Jesus remained unmoved. His bearing was marked by a certain divine dignity, while an expression of holy resignation sat upon his features. He looked like Peace, incarnate in the form of man! A soft influence seemed to flow from his presence, producing a universal but momentary emotion of sympathy. Caiaphas perceived it, and cried in his harsh, stern voice:

"'You have brought this man before me, men of Jerusalem; of what do you accuse him? Let those who have accusations come forward and make them. He is a Jew, and shall have justice by our laws.'

"'Ye Jews have no power to try a man for his life, most noble Caiaphas,' said Æmilius. 'The lives of all your nation are in the hand of Cæsar and of his tribunals. You can put no man to death.'

"Æmilius had spoken in hopes that if Jesus could be brought before Pilate, the Procurator, he might be by him released, for he knew Pilate had no envy or feeling against the Prophet.

"'Thou sayest well, noble Roman,' answered Caiaphas, 'but for the crime of blasphemy against the Temple we are permitted by Cæsar to judge our people by the laws of Moses. And this man, if rumor comes nigh the truth, has been guilty of blasphemy. But we will hear the witnesses.'

"Hereupon several of the chief priests and scribes who had been going in and out among the crowd, brought forward certain men whose very aspect showed them to be of the baser sort. One of these men testified that he had heard Jesus say that he would destroy the Temple and could again in three days rebuild it more magnificently than it was in the days of Solomon the Mighty.

"Upon this testimony all the priests shouted, 'Blasphemer!' and called for Jesus to be stoned to death.

"A second witness was now produced by Abijah, the most passionate of the scribes, who testified that Jesus had taught in Samaria that men would soon no longer worship in the Temple, but that the whole earth would be a temple for Jews and Gentiles.

"This was no sooner heard than some of the men gnashed at Jesus with their teeth, and but for the gestures and loud voice of the High Priest, they would have made an attempt to get him into their power.

"A third witness, a man who had been notorious for his crimes, now came up. He carried on his wrist a cock, with steel gaffs upon the spurs, as if he had just been brought up from the cock-pit to bear testimony, for such were the sort of fellows suborned by the priests. He testified that Jesus said that the day would soon come when not one stone should be left upon another of the Temple; that he had called it 'a den of thieves,' the priests 'blind guides' and 'deceivers,' the scribes 'foxes,' and the Pharisees 'hypocrites.'

"But the fourth and fifth witnesses contradicted each other, as also did others.

"Such opposite testimony perplexed and irritated Caiaphas and confounded the chief priests and scribes. The High Priest now began to perceive that Jesus would have to be released for want of testimony against him.

"'What! Galilean and blasphemer of God and his Temple, answerest thou nothing?' cried the High Priest; 'hearest thou not what these witness against thee?'

"But Jesus remained silent. Caiaphas was about to break the silence by some fierce words, when a voice was overheard the other side of the columns, on the left of the throne, where was a fireplace in which was burning a large fire, about which stood many persons. Rabbi Amos at once recognized in the violent speaker Peter, who had come in with him and John, the latter of whom, in the disguise of a priest, stood not far from Jesus, gazing tenderly upon him, and listening with the most painful interest to all that they testified against him; but Peter stood farther off, by the fire, yet not less eagerly attending to all that passed.

"'Thou art one of the Nazarene's followers!' cried the voice of a maid, who brought wood to feed the fire. 'Thou needest not to deny it. I am of Galilee, and knew thee when thou wert a fisherman. Seize him, for he is one of them!'

"'Woman, I swear by the altar and ark of God, and by the sacred Tables. I know not the fellow! I never saw Galilee!'

"'Thy speech betrayeth thee, now thou hast spoken!' cried the woman; 'thou art a Galilean, and thy name is Simon Bar-Jona. I know thee well, and how, three years ago, you and your brother Andrew left your nets to follow this Nazarene!'

"'May the thunders of Horeb and the curse of Jehovah follow me, if what thou sayest be true, woman. Thou mistakest me for some other man. I swear to you, by the head of my father, men and brethren, that I never saw his face before! I know not the man!'

"As he spoke," said John, "he cast his angry looks towards the place where Jesus stood. He caught his Master's eyes bent upon him, with a tender and reproving gaze, so full of sorrowing compassion, mingled with forgiveness, that I saw Peter start as if smitten with lightning. He then pressed his two hands to his face and, uttering a cry of anguish and despair that made the High Priest look, and which went to every heart, he rushed out by the open door into the darkness and disappeared. As he did so the cock, which was held tied upon the wrist of the third witness, crowed twice in a loud tone. I then remembered the words of Jesus to Peter, spoken but twelve hours before: 'This night, even before the cock crow the first watch of the morning, thou shalt thrice deny that thou knowest me!' Upon this," added John, "my confidence in my Master came back full and strong, and I felt that he would not, could not be harmed, for he foreknew all things that could happen to him, and would yet escape death.

"At length, after great excitement and dissension among the elders, chief priests and scribes, Caiaphas placed Jesus before their great council, at their demand. Their hall adjoined his own. Here they, as well as Caiaphas, questioned him closely, and said:

"'Art thou the Christ, the Son of the Blessed? I adjure thee by the living God, tell us plainly.'

"Jesus then elevated his princely form, and bending his eyes upon the face of the High Priest, with a look so brightly celestial that Caiaphas involuntarily dropped his eyelids to the ground, answered and said:

"'Ye have said that which I am!' The expression of his countenance," says John, "seemed to shine as he had seen it in the Mount, when he was transfigured before him.

"'Men of Israel and Judah, ye hear his words!' cried the High Priest, rending down the blue lace from his ephod. 'Hear ye his blasphemy! What think ye? Need we any further witness than his own mouth?'

"'He is guilty of death!' cried Abner, in a hoarse voice, his eyes, red with being up all the night, glaring like a leopard's; and advancing to where Jesus stood bound and bleeding, he spat in his face thrice.

"This was followed by a loud outcry for his death, and several vile fellows also spat upon him and pulled him by the beard.

"'Is this Jewish justice?' cried Æmilius indignantly to Caiaphas. 'Do you condemn and kill a man without witness? Stand back, for Romans are not used to see men condemned without law. Back, fellows, or your blood will flow sooner than his for which you thirst!'

"At this determined attitude they gave back for a moment, and left Jesus standing in the midst, sad but serene.

"John ran to him and wiped the blood and uncleanness from his lips and cheeks and beard, and gave him water, which the woman who had recognized Peter compassionately brought in a ewer.

"'Master, use thy power and escape from them!' whispered John.

"'Nay, tempt me not, beloved!' he answered. 'My power is not for my deliverance, but for that of the world. For you I can do mighty works, but for myself I do nothing. I came not to save my life, but to lay it down. Mine hour is at hand!'

"'Let not a handful of Romans frighten you, men of Jerusalem!' cried Abner. 'There is not a legion in all the city. Here we are masters, if we will it! To the rescue! Let me hear the lion of Judah roar in his might, and the eagle of Rome will shriek and fly away! To the rescue!'

"'Hold, men and brethren!' cried Caiaphas, who had judgment enough to see that the first blow would be the beginning of a revolution that would bring down upon the city the Roman army quartered in Syria and end in the destruction of the nation. 'Hold, madmen!'

"But his voice was drowned amid the roar of the human tempest. Æmilius and his men were borne away on the crest of the surge and so pressed by the bodies of the Jews that they could not make use of their weapons. In the wild confusion Jesus was carried by fierce hands to the opposite end of the council chamber, while Caiaphas strove to appease the wrath of Æmilius, who insisted that the fate of Jesus should be left with Pilate the Procurator.

"When Æmilius, aided by the authority of Caiaphas, at length came where Jesus had been dragged, they found him standing blindfolded among a crowd of the basest fellows of Jerusalem, who were diverting themselves by slapping his cheeks, and asking him to tell, by his divine knowledge of all things, who did it. They would also hold money before his blinded eyes, and ask him to name its value or inscription, and when he still kept silence they struck him.

"'We will let thee go, Nazarene,' said one, 'if thou wilt tell how many hairs I have in my beard.'

"'Nay, let him divine,' cried another, 'what I gave for my Passover lamb in the market, and the name of the Samaritan of whom I bought it!'

"'Out with your lambs, Kish!' shouted a third fellow, thrusting himself forward; 'let me hear him prophesy! What, Galilean! silent and sullen! I will make thee speak!' and he let a blow of his staff fall upon the head of Jesus which would have struck him to the earth, but for the voice of Caiaphas, which had arrested in part its force.

"'Men of Israel!' he cried aloud, 'that this pestilent Nazarene is a blasphemer we have heard with our ears, and by our law he ought to die, because he hath made himself the Son of God. But Cæsar hath taken the power of life and death out of our hands! We Jews can put no man to death, but the Romans only. That he hath spoken against Cæsar, and is a seditionist, can be proved. Let us take him before Pilate with this accusation!'

"This speech pleased the people, and, having rebound Jesus more securely, they cried all with one voice, 'To Pilate! To the Pretorium!'"

The multitude then poured out of the gates of the palace, like a foaming and chafing river which hath overflowed its banks, and with terrible cries, which we heard even in our house, took the direction towards the Pretorium.

It was with difficulty that Æmilius could protect the Prophet in safety up the hill and to the entrance of the Pretorium, which he entered with his prisoner just as the sun gilded the loftiest pinnacles of the Temple.

In another letter, dear father, I will continue the account of his trial, the remembrance of which, while I now write of it, almost rekindles again all my love, faith, devotion and confidence in him, for who but a man God-sustained could have borne so meekly all this pain, insult, ignominy and shame?

Adina.

LETTER XXXII.

My Dear Father:

This is the evening of the Great Day of the Feast, and the second day since the ignominious execution of him whom we all believed to have been the Christ, the Son of the Blessed. Yet he still lies dead in the tomb! Alas, that one so good and noble and wise should have been a deceiver! Henceforth I have no faith in goodness. I have wept till I can weep no more.

It is now the close of the High Day of the Feast. The slanting rays of the setting sun linger yet upon the gilded lances that terminate the lesser pinnacles of the holy house of the Lord. The smoke of incense curls lazily up from the sky from its unseen altar, and the deep voices of the choir of Levites, increased by those of the tens of thousands of Judah, who crowd all the courts of the Temple, fall upon my ears like muffled thunder. I never heard anything so solemn. Above the Temple has hung, since the crucifixion yesterday, the cloud of the smoke of the sacrifices, and it immovably depends over all the city like a pall. The sun does not penetrate it, though its light falls upon the earth outside of the city, but all Jerusalem remains in shadow. This cloud is a fearful sight, and all men have been watching it and talking of it and wondering. It seems to be in the form of black, gigantic wings, spreading a league broad over Jerusalem.

There it now hangs, visible from my window, but we are in some sort used to its dreadful presence and cease to fear; but we are lost in wonder. This morning when a high wind arose, blowing from the Great Sea eastward, every one expected and hoped to see the cloud sail away before it in the direction of the desert. But the only effect the wind produced was to agitate its whole surface in tumultuous billows, while the mass still retained its position above the city. The shadow it casts is supernatural and fearful, like the dread obscurity which marks an eclipse of the sun.

And this reminds me, my dear father, to mention what, in the multiplicity of subjects that rush to my pen for expression, I have omitted to state to you; and what is unaccountable unless men have, in truth, crucified in Jesus the very Son of God. At the time of his death the sun disappeared from the mid-heavens, and darkness, like that of night, followed over all the earth, so that the stars became visible, and the hills on which Jerusalem stands shook as if an earthquake had moved them, and many houses were thrown down; and where the dead are buried outside of the city, the earth and rocks were rent, tombs broken up, and many bodies of the dead were heaved to the surface and exposed to all eyes! These bodies have lain all to-day, for the

Jews dare not touch them to re-bury them for fear of being defiled. All this is fearful and unaccountable. It is known, too, that as Jesus expired, the vail of the Temple was rent in twain and exposed the Holy of Holies to every common gaze! What will be the end of these things is known only to the God of Abraham. Never was so fearful a Passover before. Men's faces are pale and all look as though some dread calamity had befallen the nation.

My last letter, my dear father, closed with the termination of the examination of Jesus before Caiaphas.

Guarded by Æmilius, who was his true friend to the last, he was led to the house of Pilate.

The Pretorian gates were shut by the Roman guards as the tumultuous crowd advanced, for Pilate believed the Jews were in insurrection, and was prepared to defend his palace; for so few are the troops with him in the city that he has for some weeks held only the name of power rather than the reality. But when Æmilius explained to the captain of the guard that the Jews desired to accuse Jesus, the Nazarene, of sedition before the Procurator, he was admitted, with the chief men of the city, into the outer court of Antiochus, and at their call Pilate came forth to them. When he saw the vast concourse of people with Caiaphas and the chief priests, and many rich Sadducees, with the leading men of Jerusalem in the advance, and Jesus, bound and disfigured by the insults he had undergone, and Æmilius and his few soldiers enclosing him with their protecting spears, and heard the loud voices of the multitude, as of wolves baying for the blood of a defenceless lamb, he stood with amazement for a few moments surveying the scene.

"What means this, Æmilius?" he demanded of the young Prefect. "Who is this captive?"

"It is Jesus, called the Christ, my lord, the Prophet of Galilee. The Jews desire his death, accusing him of blaspheming their God, and—"

"But I have no concern with their religion or the worship of their God. Let them judge him after their own way," said Pilate, indifferently, and with an indolent air.

"But, most noble Roman," said Caiaphas, advancing to the portico on which the Procurator stood, "by our law he should suffer death, and thou knowest, though we can condemn, as we now have done this Galilean, we have no power to execute sentence of death."

"This is well said; but would you have me put one of your nation to death for blaspheming your God? So far as that is concerned, O priest," added Pilate, smiling contemptuously, "we Romans blaspheme him daily, for we worship him not and will have naught to do with your faith. Let the man go! I see no cause of death in him!"

He then spoke to Æmilius, and desired him to lead Jesus to the spot where he stood. Pilate regarded him with mingled pity and interest. After surveying him a moment, he turned to one of his officers and said aside: "A form divine and fit for Apollo, or any of the greater gods! His bearing is like a hero! Mehercule! The chisel of Praxiteles nor of Phidias ne'er traced the outlines of limbs and neck like these. He is the very incarnation of human symmetry and dignity!"

The courtiers nodded assent to these cool criticisms of the indolent and voluptuous Italian. Jesus, in the meanwhile, stood motionless before his judge, his eyes downcast and full of a holy sadness, and his lips compressed with immovable patience. Pilate now turned to him and said:

"Thou art, then, that Jesus of whom men talk so widely. Men say, O Jesus, that thou art wiser than ordinary men; that thou canst do works of necromancy and art skilled in the subtle mysteries of astrology. I would question thee upon these things. Wilt thou read my destiny for me in the stars? If thou answerest well I will befriend thee, and deliver thee from thy countrymen who seem to howl for thy blood."

"My lord!" cried Caiaphas, furiously, "thou must not let this man go! He is a deceiver and traitor to Cæsar. I charge him and formally accuse him, before thy tribunal, with making himself king of Judea!"

To this the whole multitude assented, in one deep voice of rage and fierce denunciation that shook the very walls of the Pretorium.

"What sayest thou?" demanded Pilate, "art thou a king? Methinks if thou wert such, these Jews have little need to fear thee." And the Roman cast a careless glance over the mean and torn apparel and half-naked limbs of the Prophet.

Before Jesus could reply, which he seemed about to do, there was heard a sudden commotion in the lower part of the court of Gabbatha, and a loud, hoarse voice was heard crying:

"Make way! Give back! He is innocent!"

All eyes turned in the direction of the archway, when a man was seen forcing his path towards the door of the Judgment Hall, in front of which Pilate was standing, with Jesus a step or two below.

"What means this madman?" cried the Procurator. "Some of you arrest him!"

"I am not mad! He is innocent! I have betrayed the innocent blood!" cried Iscariot, for it was he, leaping into the space in front of the portico. "Take back thy money, and let this holy Prophet of God go free! I swear to you by the altar he is innocent, and if thou harm him thou wilt be accursed with the vengeance of Jehovah! Take back thy silver, for he is innocent!"

"What is that to us? See thou to that!" answered Abner the priest, haughtily, while the eyes of Caiaphas, falling under the withering glance of the Roman Procurator, betrayed his guilt.

"Wilt thou not release him if I give thee back the pieces?" cried Judas, in accents of despair, taking Caiaphas by the mantle and then kneeling to him imploringly.

But Caiaphas angrily shook him off. At last, in a frenzied manner, he threw himself at the knees of Jesus, and cried in the most thrilling accents:

"Oh, Master! Master! Thou hast the power! Release thyself!"

"No, Judas," answered the Prophet, shaking his head and gazing down compassionately upon his betrayer, and without one look of resentment at his having betrayed him, "mine hour is come! For this hour I came into the world!"

"I believed surely thou wouldst not suffer thyself to be arrested. It is my avarice that hath slain thee! Oh, God! Oh, God! I see now it is too late!" Thus crying in a voice of despair, he arose and rushed, with his face hid in his cloak, forth from the presence of all, towards the outer gate.

This extraordinary interruption produced a startling effect upon all present, and a few moments elapsed before Pilate could resume his examination of Jesus, which he did by entering the Judgment Hall and taking his seat on the throne. He then repeated his question, but with more deference than before: "Art thou a king, then?"

"Thou sayest that which I am—a king," Jesus answered, with a dignity truly regal in its bearing; for all the time, bound and marred as he was by the hands of his enemies, pale with suffering and with standing a sleepless and fearful night upon his feet, exposed to cold and to insults, yet he had a kingly air, and there seemed to float about his head a divine glory, as if a sunbeam had been shining down upon him.

"Thou thyself hearest him!" exclaimed Caiaphas, standing upon the threshold of the Judgment Hall of the Gentile governor, which he would not enter for fear of defilement.

"He has everywhere publicly proclaimed that he has been ordained of God to re-establish the kingdom of Judah and overthrow the power of Cæsar in

Jerusalem," added the governor of the Temple, lifting his voice so as to be heard above the voices of the priests and scribes, who, all speaking together, vehemently accused him of many other things.

Pilate at length obtained comparative silence, and then said to Jesus:

"Hearest thou these accusations? Hast thou no answer to make? Behold how many things they witness against thee!"

Pilate spoke as if he had taken a deep interest in Jesus, and would give him an opportunity of defending himself.

"He hath perverted the nation; a most pestilent and dangerous fellow!" exclaimed Caiaphas. "He is a blasphemer above all men!"

"I have nothing to do with your religion. If he hath blasphemed your gods, take ye him and judge him according to your laws," answered Pilate.

"Thou knowest, O noble Roman, that we have no power to execute to the death, therefore do we accuse him before thee."

"I am no Jew, priest! What care I for your domestic and religious quarrels? He hath done nothing that I can learn for which the laws of Imperial Rome, which now prevail here, can adjudge him to death. I, therefore, command his release."

Upon this the Jews sent up a cry of unmingled ferocity and vindictiveness. Caiaphas, forgetting his fear of defilement, advanced several steps into the Judgment Hall, and shaking his open hands at Pilate, cried:

"If thou lettest this man go, thou art not Cæsar's friend. Thou art in league with him. He that sets himself up as a king in all the wide bounds of Cæsar's dominions, wars against Cæsar, as well at Jerusalem as at Rome. If thou release this man, I and my nation will accuse thee to thy master, Tiberius, of favoring this Galilean's sedition."

When Pilate heard the name of Galilee, he asked if the prisoner were a Galilean. Upon being answered in the affirmative by the excited priests, he said to Æmilius:

"Hold! Loose not his bonds just now! Herod, the Tetrarch of Galilee, last night came up to the Passover feast of the Hebrew God, and is now at the old Maccabean Palace, with his retinue. Conduct your prisoner to him, and let Herod judge his own subjects!"

The chief priests and scribes now shouted with approbation at this decision, for they began to fear that Pilate would release Jesus, and they knew that the vacillating and reckless Herod would do whatsoever would gain popular applause.

"To Herod! To the Tetrarch of Galilee with him!" arose the cry.

But Caiaphas, frowning and dissatisfied, remained behind; and Pilate, glad to get rid of the delicate affair of condemning an innocent man, smilingly came out and spoke to the gloomy High Priest:

"Thou knowest I can condemn men only for crimes committed against the laws of the empire. This Jesus hath done nothing worthy of death."

"Noble Governor," answered Caiaphas, stopping in his angry strides up and down the porphyry floor of the outer portico, "thou forgettest that I brought him not before thee on this charge of blasphemy alone, but for sedition! By the altar of God, this is a crime known to thy laws, I wot!"

"True. You charge a young, defenceless, quiet, powerless man, destitute of money, men or arms, an obscure fisherman or carpenter of Galilee, with setting up a throne and kingdom against that of Tiberius Cæsar, the ruler of the earth! The idea is absurd! It should be treated only with ridicule. So will Herod say, when he understands the affair."

"So will not Cæsar say, my lord!" answered Caiaphas, with a sneer upon his curled lip. "If you let this man go, the Jewish nation will draw up a memorial, accusing you to the emperor of protecting treason. You will be summoned by the senate to answer the charge; and though you should succeed in clearing yourself, you will have lost your government, given to another, and for your fair name, you will live, ever after, under Cæsar's suspicion."

Pilate turned pale, and bit his lips with vexation.

"My lord priest, thou art bent, I see, on this innocent man's death. I am no Jew, to understand how he has drawn upon himself thy terrible wrath and that of thy nation. I will see what Herod will say, who, being a Jew, is familiar with your customs."

Pilate now reseated himself upon his throne to give hearing to other complaints.

After the lapse of half an hour a youth threw himself from his horse, at the door of the court, and drew near the Procurator.

"What aileth thee, Alexander?" demanded Pilate, on seeing blood on his temples and that he seemed faint.

"But a trifle now, my lord. I was thrown from my horse, who was startled at a burning torch lying on the ground, and was detained at a hospitable house until I was able to remount, which brings me hither late."

"And why come at all? What news sends my fair wife, that she should despatch you from my house in Bethany at this early hour? No evil tidings, boy?"

"None, my lord, save this note."

The Greek page then handed his master a small roll of parchment, tied with scarlet thread. He cut the knot with his dagger and reading the contents became deadly pale. Caiaphas watched him closely, as if he would read, reflected in his eyes, the contents of the note which had so deeply moved him.

"Caiaphas," said the Procurator, "this prisoner must be released!"

Jesus Before Pilate.

"It is either his destruction, proud Roman, or thine!" answered the High Priest, turning and walking haughtily away.

Pilate looked after him with a troubled air, and then re-entered the Hall of Judgment, and seating himself upon his throne, again read the parchment.

"'Have nothing to do with this just man,' he read half aloud, 'for I have suffered many things this day in a dream because of him!' The very gods seem to take sides with this extraordinary young prisoner!" he exclaimed. "Would to Jove that Herod may have sense enough to release him and relieve me of this unpleasant business."

While he was yet speaking and musing with himself, unconsciously aloud, there was heard a great noise of voices in the direction of the Maccabean Palace, and as it grew nearer and more distinct, Pilate started up and cried:

"It is as I feared—Herod gives them no satisfaction and they come again to me! Oh, that the gods would give me wisdom and nerve for this trying hour, so that I condemn not the innocent nor bring myself into the power of an accusation to Cæsar from these wicked Jews!"

At this moment the multitude, increased if it were possible in numbers and in vindictiveness, reappeared, pressing Jesus before them. This time he was alone, Æmilius having been separated from him in the palace and kept by the crowd from rejoining him. He was now unbound, and upon his head was a crown of thorns, piercing the tender temples till the blood trickled all down his face; upon his shoulders was clasped an old purple robe, once worn by Herod in his state of petty king, and his hand held a reed as a scepter; and as he walked along, the bitterest among the priests, as well as the vilest of the common fellows, mockingly bent the knee before him, crying:

"Hail, King Jesus! Hail, royal Nazarene! All hail!"

Others went before him carrying mock standards, while still others acting as heralds ran shouting:

"Make way for the King of the Jews! Do homage, all men, to Cæsar! This is the great Tiberius, Emperor of Nazareth! Behold his glittering crown! Mark his royal robes and see his dazzling sceptre! Bend the knee, bend the knee, men of Judah, before your king!"

When Pilate saw this spectacle and heard these words, he trembled and was heard to say:

"Either this man or I must perish! These Jews are become madmen with rage and demand a sacrifice. One of us must fall!"

Oh, that I could write all I feel! But I am compelled, my dear father, to end here.

Your affectionate child,

Adina.

LETTER XXXIII.

My Dear Father:

In this letter will be continued my account of the trial, if such it can be called, of Jesus.

John, the faithful and yet trusting disciple whom Jesus loved, still kept near his captive Master, and sought to cheer him by affectionate looks and, where he could do it with safety, by kind acts. More than once he was rudely thrust aside by the fiercer Jews, and once several men seized upon him and would have done him violence, if Caiaphas, to whom John is remotely related and who knows him well, had not interposed. And while John was thus doing all that he could to soften the asperity of his friend's treatment, we at home were exerting ourselves to soothe the maternal solicitude of Mary of Nazareth, his noble and heartbroken mother.

Herod, the Tetrarch of Galilee, was breaking his fast with fruit and wine, at a table overlooking by a window the Street of the Gentiles, when the noise of the advancing thousands of the Jews reached his ear. He started from the table and said:

"These people are surely up in insurrection against Pilate!"

"No, great prince," answered the lad Abel, his cupbearer, who is related to John, and has told me many of these things. "They have taken the Nazarene Prophet, Jesus, and are trying him for sedition."

"This uproar proceeds from no trial, but from a wild mob in motion, and they seem to be approaching," was his answer to him.

As Herod spoke he went to the lattice of his basilica, and beheld the head of the multitude just emerging into the street.

"There are spears and Romans in the van, and I see priests and peasants mixed together. I now see the cause of all the tumult—a mere youth, bound and soiled and pale as marble. What, sirs! this is not the great Prophet, of whose fame I have heard?" he said, turning to his officers. "What mean they by bringing him hither? Yet, Per Baccho! I am glad to get a sight of him!"

The crowd, like the swelling Nile, flowed towards the gates, roaring and chafing like its mighty cataracts, so that there was something fearfully sublime in this display of the power of human passions. Æmilius with difficulty succeeded in getting his prisoner into the piazza of the palace.

"Most royal prince," said Æmilius, kneeling before Herod and presenting a signet, "I am sent by his excellency, Pontius Pilate, the Roman Procurator of Judea, to bring before you this person accused of blasphemy. Ignorant of your customs and faith, the Governor desires that you, who are of his nation, would examine him; and moreover, Pilate, learning that he is a Galilean and a subject of your jurisdiction, courteously declines interfering with your authority."

When Herod Antipas heard delivered so courteous a message from the Procurator, with whom he had been some time at enmity, he was pleased.

"Say thou, Sir Knight, to his excellency, the most noble and princely Governor of Judea, that I appreciate his extraordinary civility, and that nothing will give me more pleasure, in return for such distinguished courtesy, than to be considered by him his friend, and that I regret any occurrence that has hitherto estranged us."

Æmilius, upon receiving this answer, arose and bowed, and then said with the boldness which characterizes him:

"Most gracious and royal Tetrarch, I pray you heed not the charges of these Jews touching this prisoner. They have conceived against him a bitter hatred without just cause. He has done nothing worthy of death. Pilate could find nothing whatsoever in him deserving of the attention of the dignity of a Roman tribunal."

"Let the prisoner fear not," answered Herod, at the same time regarding Jesus attentively as he stood before him in the calm majesty of innocence. "I will not take Pilate's prerogative of judgment out of his hand, so handsomely tendered to me. If he hath blasphemed—Mehercule! the High Priest and priests of the Temple itself," he added, laughing, "do that every day of their lives, for religion is at a low ebb among the hypocritical knaves! I have nothing to do with their charge of blasphemy, or I would have them all stoned to death without mercy. I will first see some miracles wrought by thy far-famed prisoner, noble Æmilius, and then send him back to my illustrious friend Pontius, whom his gods prosper in all things."

Herod, then, fixing his eyes curiously upon Jesus, who had stood silently before him, seemingly the only unmoved person in the vast concourse, said to the soldiers:

"Unbind him! By the staff of Jacob, he hath been roughly handled! Men of Israel, it becomes not such as you to do violence to a man before he is condemned."

While he was speaking John arranged Jesus' mantle about his form. Herod regarded with interest and looks of compassion, the pale and divinely-serene countenance of the prisoner, and seemed struck with the indescribable majesty of his aspect and bearing.

"Art thou the Nazarene Jesus, of whom I have heard so much?" he asked in deferential tones.

"I am he," was the quiet answer.

"Then gladly do I meet thee, for I have long time desired to see thee; and I would fain behold thee do some miracles. Does rumor belie thy powers? What! art thou silent? Dost thou not know who it is that speaks to thee? Come hither, fellow!" he called to a Samaritan muleteer who stood in the crowd, whose oval face and Jewish eyes showed him to be both of Assyrian and Israelitish descent, and whose arm had been taken off by a sword in a contest with Barabbas and his robbers; "come hither, and let this Prophet prove his power and mission by restoring thy arm whole like as the other!"

The man alertly came forward, and all eyes were directed eagerly upon him and upon Jesus; but he thrust the stump of his arm, by Herod's order, in vain before Jesus. The eyes of the Prophet moved not from their meditative look upon the ground.

"Art thou mocking us, thou false Christ?" cried the Tetrarch angrily. "Wilt thou neither speak nor act? If thou art not an impostor, do a miracle before us all, and we will believe in thee!"

Jesus remained motionless, yet preserved a firm and majestic countenance.

"He is a deceiver! He performed his works through Beelzebub, who has now deserted him!" cried the priests.

"Nazarene," said Herod, "I am a Jew also. If thou wilt prove to me by a sign that I will name, that thou art the Christ, I will not only become thy follower, but will let thee go free. Thy silence is an insult to my power. Thou seest yonder marble statue of Judas Maccabeus. Command the sword in its hand to wave thrice above its helmeted head, and I will bend the knee to thee. Nay, wilt not? I will give thee then, something easier to do. Seest thou the carved pomegranates in the entablature of the wall? Bid the one which hangs over this column become ripe, natural fruit, and fall at my feet. No?"

"He has no power—his friend Beelzebub hath given him up into our hands! Death to the necromancer!" were the terrible words which now made the hall tremble.

"See the whirlwind thou hast raised, O Nazarene!" cried Herod, rising. "If thou art a prophet, no harm can they do thee; and if thou art an impostor, if they kill thee thou deservest thy fate! I give thee up into their hands! Save thyself, if thou be the Christ!"

Scarcely had Herod spoken these words, relinquishing Jesus into the hands of his foes, than with a savage cry, as the famished jackals in the desert rush upon their prey, they rushed upon their victim. Æmilius could not protect him; nay, some of Herod's soldiers, whom the Jews had half intoxicated with wine, joined them as soon as they saw their master Antipas had cast him off, and began to scoff and mock him, and one of them thrust a helmet on his head and pulled the visor down over his eyes.

"Nay," said Herod on seeing this. "As he calls himself a king, remove the helmet and crown him, and robe him royally, and place a sceptre in his hand; and lo, yonder block will make him a proper throne! We must show Pilate how we Jews serve men who usurp the power of his master, Cæsar!"

One of his men of war brought a cast-off robe of purple which belonged to Herod and, with loud shouts of laughter and coarse jests, they robed him in it, unresisting as the lamb wreathed for the sacrifice. Some one then twined the creeping thorn, which grew on the outer wall, and, twisting it into the shape of a crown, handed it over the heads of the men to Abner.

When Abner saw the crown he smiled with malicious gratification and, nodding approvingly to the man said:

"This is what we needed! Nothing could have done better!" and with his two hands he placed it upon the head of Jesus, pressing cruelly the sharp thorns into his temples till the blood trickled from a dozen wounds. Jesus made no complaint, but the pain forced large bright tears from his eyes, which rolled down his cheeks and fell among the purple robe like glittering pearls.

"Here is also a sceptre for our king!" exclaimed the Samaritan with one arm, using the one to reach a piece of reed, from which a Passover lamb had been slung, to those who were arraying Jesus. This was thrust into the Prophet's grasp, and he held it patiently. His submission, his silence, his endurance of pain, his constant dignity, and the majestic submission which he seemed to manifest to all their insults and tortures, brought tears into the eyes of Æmilius. Even Herod stood amazed at such God-like forbearance, and said to his chief captain:

"If this man is not the Son of God, he is worthy to be deified! Such sublime patience is more than human—it is divine! You Romans, Æmilius, would make a hero of such a man, and when he died worship him as a god!"

"Then, mighty prince, why suffer him to be thus treated?" asked Æmilius.

"It is his own choice. I have entreated him fairly. I asked of him but one of those miracles men say he works, as proof of his Messiahship, and he works me none—shows me no sign. The inference is that he can do none, and therefore he is an impostor."

"Most royal prince," said Abner aloud, "thou now beholdest the King of the Jews, crowned, robed and sceptred!" and he pointed to Jesus.

"Hail! most puissant and potent sovereign of Galilee! Hail! King of fishermen!" cried Herod, mocking him, and seemingly greatly amused at the jest. "Hail! powerful king! What, fellows, men-at-arms and all ye gapers! bend ye not the knee before this royal personage? Do homage to your king!"

Upon this many who were around him kneeled, and some mockingly even prostrated themselves before the Prophet; but he stood so very like a monarch that others, who were about to mock him, refrained, while Herod turned away with a troubled look, saying abruptly:

"Take him back to the Procurator!"

Once more the vast multitude were in motion, and with cries and insults escorted Jesus from the presence of Herod back to the Pretorium.

When Pilate beheld their return in this manner he was greatly vexed. When once more Jesus stood before him, arrayed as I have described in the gorgeous robe and crown, Pilate, turning towards Caiaphas and the priests, said angrily:

"What more will ye have? Why bring this man again before me? Behold, I have examined him before you and have found no fault in him. Ye proved nothing by your witnesses touching those things whereof ye accuse him. I then sent you with him to Herod, and lo! the Tetrarch of Galilee, one of your own nation, finds naught in him worthy of death! Doubtless he has said something about not paying tribute, and deserves for this a light punishment, but not death. I will chastise him, charge him that he be more cautious, and let him go."

"If thou let this man go, thou art an enemy of Tiberius!" answered Caiaphas. "Seest thou what a commotion he has raised in the city? If he is released there will be a revolution."

"In the name of Olympian Jove, O Nazarene, what hast thou done to incense these Jews? If thou art their king, prove it to them or to me," demanded Pilate, greatly troubled.

"My kingdom is not of the earth," answered Jesus. "If my kingdom were an earthly one, then would my servants fight, that I should not be delivered to the Jews; but my kingdom is not of this world."

"Then thou confessest thyself a king?" exclaimed Pilate, with surprise.

"Thou sayest that which I am—a King. To this end was I born, and for this cause came I into the world, that I should bear witness to the truth."

"Truth? What is truth?" asked the Roman; but, without waiting for Jesus to reply, and seeing that the Jews outside of the hall were becoming more and more impatient, he hurriedly went out to them and said:

"I find in the prisoner no fault at all. But ye have a custom that I should at the Passover pardon a criminal out of prison, as an act of clemency, in honor of the day. Will ye, therefore, that I pardon and release unto you this 'King of the Jews'?"

No sooner had Pilate made this proposal than they all with one voice and furious gestures cried:

"No! No! Not this man! We will not have him released!"

"Barabbas! Barabbas!" was echoed and re-echoed by ten thousand voices.

This Barabbas, dear father, is the same fierce bandit of whom I have spoken, who was that day to have been crucified, with two of his lieutenants. But, at the loud demand of the people, Pilate was forced to send to the officer of the wards to let him go free.

Pilate, therefore, finding that the Jews would be content with nothing less than the blood of Jesus, returned sorrowfully into the Judgment Hall.

The residue of my narrative of the condemnation and crucifixion, I will give in the morning, dear father.

Your loving daughter,

Adina.

LETTER XXXIV.

My Dearest Father:

Jesus had from very weakness sunk upon the steps of the throne of the Hall of Judgment. John knelt by him, bathing the wounds in his temples, from off which he had boldly taken the crown of thorns. When Pilate, after giving the order to release the robber chief Barabbas, came again where Jesus was, he stopped and regarded him attentively, and with an expression of sorrow and admiration. At length he spoke:

"If thou be indeed a god, O heroic young man, as thy patience would seem to prove thee to be, thou needest not to fear these bloodhounds, that bay so fiercely for thy blood. If thou art an impostor and a seditionist, thou verily meritest death. I regard thee but as a youthful enthusiast, and would let thee go free; but I cannot protect thee. If I release thee, not only thou, but also all my troops, will be massacred, for we are but a handful in their grasp. Tell me truly, art thou a son of the divine Jupiter?"

When Jesus, instead of replying, remained silent, the Procurator said sternly:

"What! speakest thou not unto me? Knowest thou not that I have power to crucify thee as a malefactor, and power, if I choose to meet the risk, to release thee?"

Jesus looked up and calmly said:

"Thou couldst have no power against me except it were given thee from above. Therefore he that delivered me into thy hands hath the greater sin!"

And as Jesus said these words in an impressive tone, he glanced fixedly at Caiaphas, who was looking in at the door, as if designating the High Priest. Upon this Pilate pressed his hands against his forehead and paced several times to and fro before the judgment seat, as if greatly troubled. Caiaphas, seeing his irresolution, cried harshly:

"If thou lettest this self-styled king go, O Governor, thou art not Cæsar's friend!"

Pilate's brow grew dark. He took Jesus by the hand, and leading him to the portal, pointed to him, and said aloud:

"Behold your king! What will you that I should do with him? Looks he like a man to be feared?"

"We have no king but Cæsar!"

"Crucify him!"

"To the cross with the false prophet!"

"Death to the usurper! Long live Cæsar! Death to the Nazarene! To the cross! To the cross with him! Let him be crucified!"

These were the various cries from ten thousand throats that responded to the Procurator's address. Remembering the warning message sent him by his young and beautiful wife, who held great influence over him, he trembled with indecision.

"Why will you compel me to crucify an innocent man? What evil hath he done?"

"Crucify him! Crucify him!" was the deafening response.

"I will chastise him and let him go!"

"At your peril release him, O Roman!" exclaimed Caiaphas, in a menacing tone. "Either he or you must die this day for the people! Blood must flow to appease this tempest!"

When the Procurator saw that he could prevail nothing, but that rather the tumult increased, he called for water, which was brought to him in a basin by his page, and in the presence of the whole multitude he washed his hands, saying:

"I am innocent of the blood of this just person! See ye to it, O Jews, ye and your High Priest!"

"His blood be upon us, and on our children!" answered Caiaphas; and all the people re-echoed his language.

"Ay, on us and on our children rest the guilt of his blood!"

"Be it so," answered the Procurator, with a dark brow and face as pale as the dead. "Take ye him and crucify him; and may the God he worships judge you, not me, for this day's deed!"

Pilate then turned away from them and said to Jesus:

"Thou art, I feel, an innocent man, but thou seest that I cannot save thee! I know thou wilt forgive me, and that death can have no terrors for one of fortitude like thine!"

Jesus made him no answer; and Pilate, turning from him with a sad countenance walked slowly away and left the Judgment Hall. As he did so one of his captains said to him:

"Shall I scourge him, my lord, according to the Roman law, which commands all who are sentenced to die to be scourged?"

"Do as the law commands," answered the weak-minded Roman.

His disappearance was the signal for a general rush towards Jesus, chiefly by the rabble, who, indifferent about Gentile defilement, crossed the threshold into the hall, which the chief priests had refrained from doing. These base fellows seized Jesus and, aided by the men-at-arms, dragged him forth into the outer or common hall. Here they stripped him, and, by order of the chief captain, a soldier scourged him with forty stripes, save one.

All this Jesus still bore with God-like majesty. Not a murmur escaped his lips; not a glance of resentment kindled the holy depths of his eyes, which, from time to time, were uplifted to heaven, as if he sought for help and strength from thence.

Not only Æmilius but John was now separated from him; but my uncle, the Rabbi stood near, in order to see what would follow, and to use his influence, if possible, to induce the chief priests to abandon the idea of killing him.

"Good Rabbi," said Jesus to him, "let them do with me what they list. My Father hath given me into their hands. I die, but not for myself. I can keep or yield up my life, as I will."

"Oh, then, dear Master!" cried my uncle, "why not save thyself? Why shouldst thou suffer all this, and death also, if thou hast the power over thy life?"

"If I die not, then were ye all dead. The Scripture must be fulfilled which spoke of me. 'He was led like a lamb to the slaughter.'"

Here Rabbi Amos could speak no more to him, for the crowd dragged him off out of the Court of Gabbatha, and so down the steep street in the direction of the gate of the kings that leads out to Calvary, the public place of execution.

Rabbi Amos accompanied the multitude, keeping as nigh to Jesus as the Roman soldiers, who marched on each side of him, would permit. On the way, as they crossed the open space where once stood the palace and statue of Antiochus Seleucus, the eyes of the Rabbi were attracted by the cries and pointed fingers of many of the people to the body of a man lying dead at the foot of a withered fig tree. Upon drawing nearer, he recognized the features of the man Judas, who had so basely betrayed his Master. The spectacle which he exhibited was revolting and horrid to look upon! About his neck was wound a fragment of his girdle, the other half being still secured to a limb of the tree, showing how he had met his fate.

By this time the people who were dragging Jesus to death were got well beyond the gate, when a cross of heavy cypress was obtained by the centurion from a yard near the lodge. Two others were also brought out, and laid upon the shoulders of two men, the lieutenants of Barabbas, who were also that day to be crucified.

By the time the great crowd had passed the gate, it was known throughout all Jerusalem that Pilate had given orders for the crucifixion of the Nazarene Prophet; and, with one mind, all who had known him and believed in him or loved him left their houses to go out after him to witness the crucifixion; for I forgot to say that Caiaphas had promised, if Jesus were delivered up, that his followers should not be molested. Therefore every person went out of the gate towards Calvary. Mary his mother, my Cousin Mary, Martha and her sister, Lazarus, John, Peter and Thomas, and some women, relatives from Galilee, and many others, also went. When we got without the walls, we seemed to leave a deserted city behind us. As far as the eye could embrace there was a countless multitude. Jesus was borne in front, where we could now and then catch the gleam of a Roman spear. We hastened to get near him and, with difficulty, made our way to the head of the throng, both foes and friends giving back when they saw his weeping mother among us.

At the approach to Calvary we found that, from some cause, the course of the mighty current of human beings was checked. We soon learned the reason. Jesus had sunk to the ground under the weight of the wooden beams on which he was to die, and fainted.

"He is dead!" was the cry of those about him; but, as we drew near, he was just reviving, some one having offered wine to his lips and poured water upon his brow. He stood up, looking mildly around, when meeting his mother's gaze, he said touchingly:

"Weep not, my mother! Remember what I have often told thee of this hour, and believe. Mine hour is come!"

Thus speaking he smiled upon his mother and upon us, with a certain look of divine peace illuminating his countenance.

Barabbas, the robber chief, who had in some degree taken the lead of the mob, now, with the aid of three men, raised the cross again to the shoulders of Jesus, and the soldier ordered him to move on. But the young victim sank at once beneath the insupportable load. Upon this they were at a loss what to do, for it is ignominious for Jew or Gentile to aid in bearing a malefactor's cross, and not a Roman would touch it. At this crisis they discerned a Syro-Phœnician merchant, Simon of Cyrene, a venerable man, well known to all in Jerusalem. This man was for some reason particularly obnoxious to Abner, and, on seeing him, he pointed him out to the centurion as "one of the Nazarenes," and suggested that he should be compelled to bear the cross after Jesus.

The Cyrenian merchant was at once dragged from his mule and led to the place where the cross lay, believing he was about to be himself executed. But when he beheld Jesus standing, pale and bleeding, by the fallen cross, and knew what was required of him, he burst into tears and, kneeling at his feet, said:

"If they compel me to do this, Lord, think not that I aid thy death! I know that thou art a prophet come from God."

"We brought thee not here to prate, old man, but to work. Thou art strong-bodied. Up with this end of the cross and go on after him!" cried the chief priests.

Simon, who is a powerful man, though threescore years of age, raised the extremity of the beam, and Jesus essayed to move under the weight of the other; but he failed.

"Let me bear it alone, Master," answered the stout Simon. "I am the stronger. Thou hast enough to bear the weight of thine own sorrow. If it be a shame to bear a cross after thee, I glory in my shame, as would my two sons, were they here this day."

Thus speaking, he lifted the cross and bore it on his shoulders after Jesus, who, weak from loss of blood and sleep, and weary unto death, had to lean for support against one arm of the instrument of death.

Ah, my dear father, what a place was this across which we moved! Skulls lay scattered beneath our footsteps, and everywhere human bones bleached in the air, and we trod in heaps of ashes where the Romans had burned the bodies of many of those whom they crucified.

The crosses carried by the thieves were now thrown down by them; by one with an execration, by the other with a sigh, as he anticipated the anguish he was to suffer upon it.

The larger cross of the three was that for Jesus. It was taken by three soldiers from the back of the old Cyrenian merchant and cast heavily upon the earth. It was now that a crisis approached of the most painful interest. The centurion ordered his soldiers to clear a circle about the place where the crosses were to be planted with their spears. The Jews who had crowded near, in eager thirst for their victim's blood, gave back slowly and reluctantly before the sharp points of the Roman lances pushed against their breasts, for the centurion had with him full threescore men-at-arms, besides a part of Herod's guard. John, however, held his place close by his

Master. He relates that Jesus continued to evince the same sublime composure when the centurion commanded the crucifiers to advance and nail the malefactors to their crosses. The robber-lieutenant, Ishmerai, who was an Edomite, upon seeing the man approach with the basket containing the spikes and hammers, scowled fiercely upon him and looked defiance. He was instantly seized by four savage-looking Parthian soldiers of the Roman guard, and stripped and thrown upon his back upon the cross. His struggles, for he was an athletic man, were so violent that it took six persons to keep him held down upon the arms of the cross and his palms spread open to receive the entering nail, which one of the crucifiers, with naked and brawny arms, pressing one knee upon the wrist, drove in through the flesh and wood, by three quick and powerful blows with his short, heavy-headed hammer.

Thus secured he was left, bleeding and writhing, by the six crucifiers; for there are four to bind the victim, one to hold the spikes, and the sixth to drive them home with his hammer, and from the glance I caught of their half-naked and blood-stained figures, they were worthy to hold the dreadful office which made all men shun them as if they were leprous.

They now approached Omri, the other robber, who was a young man with a mild look, and a face whose noble lineaments did not betray his profession. He was the son of a wealthy citizen in Jericho, and had by riotous living, spent his patrimony and joined Barabbas. He had heard Jesus preach in the wilderness of Jordan, and had once asked him with deep interest many things touching the doctrines he taught.

When the crucifiers, with their cords, basket, nails and iron hammer, drew near him, he said:

"I will not compel you to throw me down. I can die as I have lived, without fear. As I have broken the laws, I am ready to suffer the penalty of the laws."

Thus speaking, he stretched himself upon his cross and, extending his palms along the transverse beam, he suffered them to nail him to the wood, uttering not a moan. He glanced towards Jesus at the same time with an expression of courage, as if he sought to show him that the pain could be borne by a brave man. And perhaps, indeed, Jesus looked as if he needed an heroic example before him to show him how to die without shrinking, for his cheek was like the marble of Paros in its whiteness, and he seemed ready to drop to the earth from weakness. His youth, his almost divine beauty, which not even his tangled hair and torn beard and blood-streaked countenance could wholly hide, the air of celestial innocence that beamed from his eyes, drew upon him many glances of sympathy even from some of his foes. The centurion, who was a tall man with a grizzly beard, and with the hardy exterior of an old Roman warrior, looked upon him with a sad gaze and said:

"I do not see what men hate thee for, for thou seemest more to be a man of love; but I must do my duty, and I hope thou wilt forgive me what I do. A soldier's honor is to obey."

Jesus smiled forgiveness upon him so sweetly that the stern Roman's eyes filled with tears, and he placed his gauntleted hand to his face to conceal his emotion.

But, my dear father, I can go on no longer now with my sad narrative. I am weary weeping at the recollections it calls before me, and at our present affliction. In my next I will complete my account of the unhappy crucifixion of the Prophet of Nazareth.

Your affectionate daughter,

Adina.

_____

LETTER XXXV.

Jerusalem—Third Morning after the Crucifixion.

My Dear Father:

As I resume my pen by the faint light of the dawn, to continue the particulars of the crucifixion of the unhappy son of Mary, who, widowed and childless, still remains with us, mourning over her dead son, my heart involuntarily shrinks from the painful subject and bleeds afresh. But there is a fascination associated with all that concerns him, even now that he is dead and has proved himself as weak a mortal as other men, which urges me to write of him and which fills my thoughts only with him.

I have just alluded to his grief-smitten mother. Alas, there is no consolation for her! Her loss is not like that of other mothers. Her son has not only been taken from her by death, but has died ignominiously on a Roman cross, executed between two vile malefactors, as if he himself were the greatest criminal of the three; and not only this, but executed as a false prophet—as a deceiver of Israel.

Yet her love for her son—that deathless, maternal love, which seems immortal in its nature—is not buried with him. She, with dearest Mary and Martha, has just gone out secretly, before the Jews are astir, to pay the last duties to his dead body, ere we all depart for an asylum in Bethany. Until they return from this sad mission of love I will continue my subject—the crucifixion.

When the centurion to whom was committed by Pilate the charge of conducting the crucifixion of Jesus, gave orders to bind him also to the cross, which lay upon the ground like an altar awaiting its victim, the four Parthian soldiers, his brutal crucifiers, laid hold upon him and began to strip him of his garments, for his enemies had put again on him his own clothes when they led him out of the hall of Pilate. He wore a mantle woven without seam by Mary and Martha, and which had been a present to him by the sisters, as a token of their gratitude, for raising from the dead their brother Lazarus.

His mother, supported by John, could no longer gaze upon her son, and was borne afar off, crying thrillingly:

"Oh, let me not hear the crashing of the nails into his feet and hands! My son! My son! Oh, that thou wouldst now prove to thy mother that thou art a true Prophet!"

"What means this wailing?" cried the fierce Abner. "Who is this woman?"

"The mother of Jesus," I answered, indignantly.

"The mother of the blasphemer! Let her be accursed!" he cried, in a savage tone. "Thou seest, woman, what is the end of bringing up an impostor, to blaspheme Jehovah and the Temple. Thy hopes and his, O wretched woman, have this day miserably perished! So die all false Christs and false prophets!"

Mary buried her face in her hands and wept on my shoulder. I could not look towards the place where Jesus stood. I dreaded to hear the first blow upon the dreadful nails, and as she stopped her ears I would have closed mine also, but that my hands supported her. I could hear the awful preparations—the rattling of the hard cord, as they bound him to the cross, and the low, eager voices of the four busy Parthians, and then the ringing of the spikes, and then silence like that of the grave! Suddenly a blow of a hammer broke the moment of suspense! A shriek burst from the soul of the mother that echoed far and wide among the tombs of Golgotha!

I could see, hear no more!

John having left the stricken mother with me, he and Lazarus had gone back to where they were unrobing the Prophet in order to bind him to the wood. They caught the eyes of their Master, said Lazarus, who gazed upon them calmly and affectionately. They said they had never beheld him appear so majestic and great. He looked, as the centurion afterwards said, "Like a god surrendering himself to death for the safety of his universe!"

"Nothing but the ferocious madness of the chief priests and Jews," added John, "could have prevented them from being awed by the majesty of his presence. And, besides, there sat upon his brow heroic courage, with a certain divine humility and resignation. Not the rough hands of the barbaric soldiers, nor the indignity of being stripped before the eyes of thousands, not the sight of the cross, nor of the thieves, nailed and writhing on theirs, moved him to depart, by look or bearing, from that celestial dignity which, through all, had never left him.

"He made no resistance," continued John, who told me what follows, "when bound upon the cross, but resigned himself passively into the hands of his executioners, like a lamb receiving its death. 'Father,' he said, raising his holy eyes to heaven, 'forgive them, for they know not what they do.'

"Great drops of sweat, when they nailed his feet to the wood, stood upon his forehead," added John, who remained near to see his Master die, and to comfort and strengthen him; "and when the four men raised him and the cross together from the earth and let the end into a hole a foot deep, the shock, bringing his whole weight upon the nails in his hands, tore and lacerated them, nearly dislocating the shoulders at the same time, while every sinew and muscle of his arms and chest was drawn out like cords to sustain this unwonted weight upon them. The first thief fainted from pain, at the shock caused by the setting of his own cross; and the second, cool and defiant as he had been, uttered a loud outcry of agony. But Jesus made no moan, though the unearthly pallor of his countenance showed how inexpressible was his torture."

Ah, my dear father, I would draw a veil over this scene—for it is too painful for me to dwell upon. To the last John believed his Master would not die—that he would not suffer! But when he saw how that pain and anguish seized heavily upon him, and how that he suffered like other men, without power to prevent it, he greatly wondered, and began to believe that all the miracles that he had seen him perform must have been illusions. He could not reconcile the calmness and dignity, the heroic composure and air of innocence with which he came to the cross, with imposture; yet his death would assuredly seal as imposture all his previous career.

With his mother we all drew as near the cross as we were permitted to come. Jesus then turned his head towards his mother, and, looking down with the profoundest tenderness and love upon her, committed her to the filial care of the weeping John, who stood supporting her.

There we waited, in expectation of seeing him do some mighty miracle from the cross and descend unharmed, showing to the world thereby his title to be the Messias of God.

The centurion, having placed a guard about the crosses, to keep the friends of the crucified from attempting their rescue, stood watching them. The soldiers who had nailed Jesus to the tree now began to divide, with noisy oaths, his garments among themselves, as well as those of the two thieves, these being by the Roman law the fee of the executioner. This division being made after some time, but not without high talking and drawing of their long Syrian knives upon each other, they were at a loss what to do with the large mantle without seam, which the sisters of Lazarus had woven for the friend of their once dead brother. A group of the Roman guard being seated near, astride upon the four arms of a fallen cross, playing at dice, suggested that the Parthians should decide by lot whose it should be. This the latter consented to and, taking the dice-box in their bloody hands, each of them threw the dice. The highest number fell to the most ferocious of the four fellows, who proposed to sell the cloak, which John joyfully purchased of him at a great price, by means of the jewels of several of the women, who gladly took rings from their ears and bracelets from their arms, I giving, dear father, the emerald which you bought for me at Cairo. But I could not see the robe which Jesus had worn thus desecrated.

After Jesus had hung about an hour upon the cross, Æmilius came from Pilate, and bore the inscription, which it is usual to place above the heads of malefactors, showing their name, and the crime for which they are crucified.

Above the head of Jesus, by means of a small ladder, was placed this inscription, in Greek, Latin, and Hebrew:

THIS IS JESUS,
THE KING OF THE JEWS.

When the wicked Abner read this, he turned angrily to the centurion, and to Æmilius, who stood sadly near the cross.

"Write not, O Roman, that he is 'King of the Jews,' but that he said he was King of the Jews!"

"I have placed above him what Pilate has ordered to be written," answered the centurion.

Abner, upon this, mounted a mule and hastened into the city to the Procurator, and laid his complaint before him.

"What I have written, I have written, sir priest," we have heard that the Procurator coldly answered.

"But you, then, have crucified this man for being our king, which we deny!" retorted Abner.

"I will take his word, before that of all the Jews in Cæsar's empire!" answered Pilate angrily. "He said he was a king; and if ever a king stood before a human tribunal, I have had a true and very king before me to-day—and I have signed the warrant for his execution. But his blood be on your heads! Leave my presence, Jew!"

Abner left his presence abashed, and returned to the place of crucifixion. The Jews, in the meanwhile, mocked Jesus, and wagged their heads at him, and reminded him of his former miracles and prophecies.

"Thou that raisedst Lazarus, save thyself from death!" said a Pharisee.

"If thou art the Son of God, prove it by coming down from the cross!" cried the leader of the Sadducees, Eli.

"Thou who saidst if a man kept thy sayings he should never see death—let us see if thou canst avoid death thyself!" said Iddo, the chief of the Essenes.

"He saved others—himself he cannot save!" mocked Ezekias, one of the chief priests.

Æmilius, finding it impossible to save the Prophet from crucifixion, had come out to guard him from the usual insults of the rabble, while he was dying. He had now lost faith in Jesus as a Jewish Prophet, but he loved him still as a man, and pitied him for his sufferings. He talked with him, and earnestly prayed him, as he hung, if he were indeed a god, to show his power! Jesus at first made no reply; but he shortly said, in a faint voice:

"I thirst."

The generous knight ran and filled a sponge with the preparation of sour wine and hyssop, usually given to malefactors, after they have suffered awhile, in order to stupefy them, and render them insensible to their sufferings. While Æmilius was affixing a sponge, dipped in this vessel of vinegar, upon a reed, split at the end to hold it firmly, Ishmerai, the robber, who all the while, as he hung, had uttered execrations upon his crucifiers, and upon Pilate, called, howling fiercely, to Jesus:

"If thou be the Son of God, save thyself and us! If thou didst raise a man once from the dead, thou canst surely keep us from dying! Thou art a vile wretch if thou hast power as a prophet, and will not use it for me, when thou seest how heavy I am of body, and how my great weight tortures me, with infernal racking and rending of every joint."

But Omri, rebuking his fellow, said:

"Dost thou not fear God, seeing thou art in the same condemnation? We suffer justly for our crimes, and to-day do receive the due reward of our transgressions; but this young man hath done nothing amiss, save to preach against the wickedness of the priests, and for being holier than they. Lord, I believe that thou art the Son of God! None but the Christ could do the works that thou hast done, or suffer patiently as thou art doing. Lord, remember me when thou comest into thy kingdom."

Jesus turned his bleeding head towards him, and, with a smile of ineffable glory radiating his pale face, said:

"Verily, I say unto thee, this day shalt thou be with me in Paradise."

Omri, upon this, looked inexpressibly happy, and seemed to rise superior to his sufferings. The other cursed the Prophet aloud, and gnashed at him with his teeth, with looks of demoniacal hatred.

At this moment Æmilius came near with his dripping sponge, and presented the reed upwards to the parched lips of the suffering Jesus. When he tasted it, he would not drink, for he perceived it was the opiate which was usually administered in compassion, to shorten the anguish of the crucified.

The robber, Ishmerai, now eagerly cried for the oblivious sponge, and the Prefect giving the reed to a soldier, the latter placed it to the mouth of the robber, whose swollen tongue protruded! He drank of it with a sort of mad thirst. The other man, also, gladly assuaged his burning fever with it, and soon afterwards both of them sunk into insensibility.

All at once, just as the sixth hour was sounded from the Temple, by the trumpets of the Levites, the cloud which, formed by the smoke of the numerous sacrifices, had hung all day above the Temple, was seen to become suddenly of inky blackness, and to advance towards Calvary, spreading and expanding in the most appalling manner, as it approached us; and in a few minutes, not only all Jerusalem, but Calvary, the Valley of Kedron, the Mount of Olives, and all the country, were involved in its fearful darkness. The sun, which had before been shining with noonday brilliancy, became black as sackcloth of hair, and a dreadful, unearthly, indescribable night overshadowed the world! Out of the center of the cloud, above the crosses, shot forth angry lightnings in every direction. But there was no thunder attending it—only a dead, sepulchral, suffocating silence!

Of the thousands who had been gazing upon the crucifixion, every one was now fallen prostrate upon the earth in terror! Jerusalem was blotted out from our view; only an angry spot of fire-red light, as it were the terrible eye of God itself, was visible above the Temple, over the place of the Holy of Holies. The crosses were no longer visible, save by the fearful shine of the lightnings, flashing fiercely from the dread and silent cloud. The form of Jesus, amid the universal gloom, shone as if divinely transfigured, and a soft halo of celestial light encircled his brow like a crown of glory; while the dark bodies of the two robbers could scarcely be discerned, save by the faint radiance emanating from his own.

Men talked to each other in whispers. An indefinable dread was upon each mind; for the sudden overspreading of the darkness was as unaccountable as it was frightful. Mary, his mother, and Lazarus, exclaimed with awe, both speaking together:

"This is his power. He has produced this miracle!"

"And we shall behold him next descend from the cross," cried Rabbi Amos. "Let us take courage!"

Three hours—three long and awful hours, this supernatural light continued—and all that while the vast multitude remained fixed, and moaning, waiting they knew not what! At length the cloud parted above the cross, with a loud peal of thunder, while a shower of terrible lightning fell, like lances of fire, all around the form of Jesus, which immediately lost its halo and its translucent radiance, His face, at the same time, became expressive of the most intense sorrow of soul.

A hundred voices exclaimed, with horror:

"See! he is deserted, and punished by the Almighty!"

We ourselves were amazed and appalled. Our rising hopes were blasted by the livid lightnings, which seemed to blast him! Heaven, as well as man, seemed to war against him! His mother gave utterance to a groan of agony, and sank upon the ground, satisfied that her son was truly accursed of God. At this moment, as if to confirm all our fears, he cried, in the Hebrew tongue:

"Eloi! Eloi! My God, my God, why hast thou forsaken me?"

Upon this, some, pitying his sufferings, ran to give him wine and hyssop, to deaden them.

"Nay, let him live—let us see if Elias will save him!" answered Abner. "He calleth for Elisha the prophet!"

Suddenly the darkness, which had filled all the air, seemed now to concentrate and gather about the cross, so that he who hanged thereon, became invisible. From the midst of it his thrilling voice was once more heard, as clear and strong as it rang over the waters of Galilee when he preached from a boat to the thousands thronging the shore:

"It is finished! Father, into thy hands I commend my spirit!"

As he uttered these words, a supernatural glory shone around him, and, with a deep sigh, he bowed his head upon his breast and gave up the ghost!

The general exclamation of surprise that followed these clear trumpet-tones, was suddenly checked by a terrible trembling of the earth beneath our feet, so that vast numbers of people were cast down; the rocks of Calvary were rent, and thrown upwards, while the whole city shook with the convulsive throes of an earthquake. The Temple seemed on fire, and above its pinnacle appeared a flaming sword, which seemed to us to cleave the walls to their foundations; and while we looked, the sword changed into the shape of a cross of dazzling light, standing high in the air, over the altar; and from its golden beams poured rays so bright, that all Jerusalem, and the hill country for a wide extent, became as light as noon-day. The ground still continued to rock, and the sepulchres of the kings, with the tombs of ancient prophets, were riven by vast chasms, and the green earth was strewn with the bones and bodies of the dead. The dark cloud, which had begun to form first with the smoke of the sacrifices of the Temple, was now dissipated by the light of the fiery cross, and the sun reappeared. Before it the glorious vision over the Temple gradually faded out and disappeared. The natural order of things gradually returned; and men, smiting their breasts, began to move towards the city, filled with awe and dread at what they had witnessed. The centurion, who stood watching these fearful things, said, aloud, to Æmilius:

"This man spake the truth. He was a god!"

"Truly," responded Æmilius, "this was none other than the Son of God— the very Christ of the Jewish Prophets. All things in the air and on the earth sympathize with his death, as if the God of nature had expired."

Sad and weeping, we left the dismal scene, hanging our heads in despondency; having, even while wondering at these mighty events connected with his crucifixion, abandoned, forever, all hope that this was he who should have redeemed our nation and restored the royal splendor of Judah and the throne of the house of David.

I am, my dear father, your loving daughter,

Adina.

LETTER XXXVI.

Jerusalem—Third Morning after the Crucifixion.

My Dear Father:

On the day on which the wonderful events took place which I have detailed at large in my last letter, the chief priests, at the head of whom was Annas, met Pilate as he was riding forth from the city, attended by a score of men-at-arms, to survey the deep rents made by the earthquake, and to hear from the mouths of all the people the particulars of the marvels which attended the crucifixion of Jesus. When they came near him, they besought him that he would command his soldiers to take down the bodies, as the next day was a high-day, and that it was contrary to their customs to have criminals executed or left hanging on that day.

"What think ye?" demanded Pilate, reining up and soothing his Syrian war-horse, which, startled at the dead bodies that lay near (for they were crossing the place of the opened tombs), had for some time tramped and plunged madly. "What think ye, priests! Have ye crucified a man or a god? We think these mighty wonders tell us that he was more than a man!"

The priests looked troubled, and seemed unable to answer. But Terah, chief priest of the house of Mariah, answered and said:

"My lord, these were wonderful phenomena, but they would have happened if this Nazarene had not died! Here is a famous astrologer from Arabia, who studies the skies, who says that this darkness was caused by an eclipse of the sun! The dark cloud was but the smoke of the sacrifices, while the earthquake was but a natural and usual occurrence!"

"Stay, sir priest," answered Pilate; "we at Rome, though called barbarians by you polished Jews, have some scholarship in astrology. We know well that an eclipse of the sun can take place only when the moon is new! It is to-day, on this eve of the high-day, at its full, and will to-night rise nearly opposite the sun! It was no eclipse, sir priest, and thy Arabian is a false astrologer. These events occurred because that divine man, your king, has been executed."

Thus speaking, the Roman Procurator spurred on towards the place, followed by his body-guard; now avoiding an open grave, now leaping one of the freshly opened chasms, now turning aside from some body cast up by the earthquake. When he came in front of the crosses, he saw that Jesus hung as if dead, while the thieves still breathed and from time to time heaved groans of anguish, although partly insensible from the effects of the opiate which had been administered to them.

"Think you, Romulus, that he has any life in him?" asked Pilate, in a subdued tone of voice, gazing sorrowfully, and with looks of self-reproach, upon the drooping form of his victim.

"He is dead an hour ago," answered the centurion. "He expired when the earthquake shook the city, and the flaming sword was unsheathed in the air above the Temple! It was a fearful sight, sir, and the more wonderful to see it change in the shape of a cross of fire. I fear, sir, we have crucified one of the gods in the shape of a man."

"It would appear so, centurion," answered Pilate, shaking his head. "I would it had not been done! But 'tis past! The Jews desire their bodies to be removed before their great Sabbath. Let them have their desire."

Pilate then turned his horse and rode slowly and sadly away from the spot. Romulus gave orders to his soldiers to remove the bodies. When the soldiers came to Jesus they saw that he was already dead.

"Let us not break his legs," said one to the other; "it were sacrilege to mar such a manly form."

"Yet we must insure his death, ere he can be taken away," responded the other. "I will pierce him to make sure!"

Thus speaking, the soldier directed his spear to the side of Jesus, and cleaved the flesh to his heart. John, who stood near, and saw and heard all, upon seeing this done bowed his head to the earth in total abandonment of hope!

When he raised his head to gaze upon his crucified Master, he saw flowing from the rent in his side two fountains together, one of crimson blood, and lo! the other of crystal water! He could not believe what he saw, until the soldiers and the centurion expressed aloud their wonder at such a marvel.

"Never was such a man crucified before," exclaimed the centurion.

In the meanwhile, Rabbi Joseph, the counsellor of Arimathea, who stands high in favor with Pilate, met the Governor as he was skirting the wall of the city with his cohort, and asked him if, after Jesus should be pronounced dead, he might take down the body and give it sepulchre.

"Go and receive the body of this wonderful man," said Pilate. "Methinks thou art one who knew him well. What thinkest thou of him, Rabbi?" Joseph perceived that Pilate asked the question with deep interest, seemingly very greatly troubled in mind, and he answered him boldly:

"I believe that he was a Prophet sent from God, your excellency, and that to-day has died on Calvary the most virtuous, the wisest, and the most innocent man in Cæsar's empire."

"My conscience echoes your words," answered Pilate, gloomily; and putting spurs to his horse, he galloped forward in the direction of the Gethsemane Gardens.

Proceeding to the cross, Joseph, by the aid of Lazarus, Simon Peter, Mary, Martha, and Rabbi Amos, took it out of the socket in the rock, with its precious burden, and gently laid it upon the ground with the body still extended upon it.

In the still, holy twilight of that dread day, the west all shadowy gold and mellow light, the air asleep, and a sacred silence reigning in heaven and on earth, they bore away from the hill of death the body of the dead Prophet. The shoulders of Nicodemus, of Peter, of Lazarus, and of John, gently sustained the loving weight of Him they once honored above all men, and whom, though proved by his death, as they believed, to have fatally deceived himself as to his divine mission as the Christ, they still loved for his sorrows so patiently borne, for his virtues so vividly remembered.

Slowly the little group wound their way along the rocky surface of Golgotha, the last to leave that fearful place in the coming darkness. Their measured tread, their low whispers, the subdued wail of the women who followed the rude bier of branches, the lonely path they trod, all combined to render the spectacle one of touching solemnity. The shades of evening were gathering thick around them. They took secret ways for fear of the Jews. But some that met them turned aside with awe when they knew what corpse was borne along, for the impression of the appalling scenes of the day had not yet wholly passed away from their minds. At length they reached a gate in the wall of the garden attached to the noble abode of the wealthy Rabbi Joseph, who went before, and with a key unlocked it, and admitted them into the secluded enclosure. Here the thickness of the foliage of olive and fig trees created complete darkness; for by this time the evening star was burning like a lamp in the roseate west. They rested the bier upon the pavement beneath the arch, and awaited in silence and darkness the appearance of torches which Rabbi Joseph had sent for to his house. The servants bearing them were soon seen advancing, the flickering light from the flambeaux giving all things visible by it a wild aspect, in keeping with the hour.

"Follow me," said Joseph, in a low voice, that was full charged with deep sorrow, as the servants preceded him with their torches.

The sad bearers of the dead body of Jesus raised their sacred burden from the ground, and trod onward, their measured foot-falls echoing among the aisles of the garden. At its farther extremity, where the rock hangs beetling over the valley, and forms at this place the wall of the garden, was a shallow flight of stone steps leading to a new tomb hewn out of the rock. It had been constructed for the Rabbi himself, and had just been completed, and in it no man had ever been laid.

The servants, by command of Joseph, rolled back the stone, and exposed the dark vault of the gaping sepulchre.

"How is it, most worthy Rabbi," said a Roman centurion, suddenly apprizing them of his presence by his voice, "that you bury thus with honor a man who has proved himself unable to keep the dazzling promises he has allured so many of you with?"

All present turned with surprise at seeing not only the centurion, but half a score of men-at-arms, on whose helmets and cuirasses the torches brightly gleamed, marching across the grass towards the spot.

"What means this intrusion, Roman?" asked Rabbi Joseph.

"I am sent hither by command of the Procurator," answered the centurion; "the chief Jews have had an interview with him, informing him that the man whom he had crucified had foretold that after three days he would rise again. They, therefore, asked a guard to be given them to place over the sepulchre, till the third day, lest his disciples secretly withdraw the body, and report that their master is risen. Pilate, therefore, has commanded me to keep watch to-night with my men."

"We bury him with this deference and respect, centurion," answered Rabbi Joseph, "because we believe him to have been deceived, not a deceiver. He was gifted by God with vast power, and therefore doubtless believed he could do all things. He was too holy, wise, and good to deceive. He has fallen a victim to his own wishes for the weal of Israel which were impossible by man to be realized."

The body of Jesus, wrapped in its shroud of spotless linen, and surrounded by the preserving spices of Arabia, was then borne into the tomb, and laid reverently upon the table of stone which Joseph had prepared for his own last resting-place. Simon Peter was the last to quit the side of the body, by which he knelt as if he would never leave it, shedding all the while great tears of bitter grief. John only, at last, drawing him gently forth, enabled the centurion and soldiers to close the heavy door of the tomb. Having secured it evenly by revolving it in its socket, the signet-bearer of the Procurator, who had come with the soldiers, placed a mass of wax, melted by a torch, upon each side of it over the crevices, and stamped each with the Imperial signet, which to break is death!

The Jews who were present, seeing that the sepulchre was thus made sure by the sealing of the stone, and by the setting of the vigilant Roman watch of eighteen men, took their departure. Rabbi Joseph, Nicodemus, and the rest of the friends of Jesus, then slowly retired, leaving a sentinel pacing to and fro before the tomb, and others grouped about beneath the trees or on the steps of the sepulchre, playing at their favorite game of dice, or gazing upon the broad moon, conversing, or singing their native Italian airs; yet with their arms at hand, ready to spring to their feet at the least alarm or word of alert.

(Something fearful must this instant have happened, for the house has just shaken as if with an earthquake. What can be the meaning of these wonders?)

This morning Mary and Martha, with others, have gone to visit Jesus' tomb in Joseph's garden (as I have already said), for the purpose of embalming the body, and on their return we are to go to Bethany for a few days, until the violent hostility of the Jews to his followers subsides.

I hear now the voices of Mary and Martha, in the court of the street, returning from the tomb. They are pitched to a wild note of joy! What can mean the commotion—the exclamations—the running, and shouting, all through the corridors and court? I must close, and fly to learn what new terror or wonder has occurred.

In haste, your affectionate daughter,

Adina.

LETTER XXXVII.

Jerusalem—First Day of the week.

My Dear Father:

How shall I make known to you, in words, the marvelous, joyous, happy, happy, and most wonderful news which I have to tell! My heart beats, my hand trembles with rapture, while a sense of profound awe impresses all my soul! Jesus is alive! Jesus has risen from the dead! Jesus has proved himself to be the Son of God!

I can scarcely hold my pen for joy and wonder, or collect my thoughts, for very amazement, at what has transpired.

Upon hearing my name called by Mary, and others, in eager, joy-trembling tones, I hastened to go down. On reaching the staircase I met my cousin ascending, almost flying. Wonder, love, and happiness inexpressible, beamed from her beautiful countenance. Meeting me, she threw her arms about my neck and essayed to utter something! But her heart was too full, and, bursting into sobs, she wept convulsively upon my bosom, in an ecstasy of delirious joy.

Amazed and confounded, not knowing what had happened, I held her to my heart, and tried to soothe her emotion.

"What—oh, what hath happened? Speak, dear Mary!" I asked, unable to wait longer in suspense.

She raised her head, and through her tears and smiles, at length said, brokenly:

"He—he—is—risen—oh, he is risen from the tomb!"

"Who?" I cried, half believing, yet doubting.

"The Lord! Our Mighty Master—Jesus—the very Son of God, the Blessed! He is alive, Adina! Come—delay not! I have flown into the city to tell thee, and Mary has told Peter and John, whom she met at the door, and who, doubting, as thou hast done, have run to see if these things be so. They will find the sepulchre empty! Haste to go with us!"

While, overwhelmed with wonder, and trembling with joy, I was preparing to accompany her, Martha appeared, her face radiant with celestial happiness.

"You have heard the tidings of great joy, O Adina?"

"Can they be true, Martha?" I asked, earnestly.

"Yes, for I have seen him walking, heard his voice, and touched him! You, also, shall see him, for he hath sent us to tell his disciples!"

I wept for joy!

At the gateway we met Mary of Bethany, and we three now hastened together towards the garden of Joseph, I wishing my feet wings, that I might reach the sepulchre sooner, fearing that the vision of Jesus would be vanished ere I arrived. As we were going out of the gate, we were met by four or five Roman soldiers, who, with aspects stamped with fear, were running past us into the city.

"What means this flight and terror, men?" cried the captain of the gate. "You fly as if you were in full retreat from an enemy. Speak, Marius! You seem to have your senses!" he demanded of the youngest of the soldiers, an officer under a centurion.

We paused to hear what he said.

"Per Dian, captain! we have been terrified beyond measure," answered the soldier. "My heart beats yet, as if it were an alarum-drum. You see, we were a part of the guard left in charge of the sepulchre of this Jewish Prophet, crucified three days ago. Before dawn this morning, as I was pacing to and fro before the tomb, there suddenly shone round about us a light, like a descending meteor, accompanied by a rushing as if of a legion of wings. The men started to their feet in amazement! On looking about us I saw a dazzling form, in the mid-heavens, with broad wings of gold, sparkling with myriads of stars, every feather a star, and clad in raiment white and gleaming as the summer's lightning. This terrible presence, like that of one of the Dii Immortales, made us fear exceedingly, beyond any terror we had before experienced. But when we saw this mighty being descend straight towards the tomb, and beheld the resplendent majesty of his celestial visage, which blinded us, our hearts failed within us. The angel, or god, alighted amid a blaze of radiance at the door of the sepulchre; and as his foot touched the earth it trembled, as if with a great earthquake. The soldiers shook with terror, and fell to the ground, before his presence, as dead men. I stood, unable to move, frozen by fear to a statue. He touched the great stone door with one of his fingers, and it rolled outward at his feet, as if a catapult had struck it, and, like Jove taking his throne, he sat upon it!

"But one thing more," continued the soldier, "was wanting to fill my cup of terror to the full. And it followed. I saw the crucified Prophet rise up from the slab on which he was laid, and stand upon his feet, and walk forth alive, with the tread of some mighty conqueror! The celestial being, so terrible in his majestic splendor, veiled his face with his wings before his presence, and prostrated himself at his feet, as if in homage to one greater than himself!

"I saw no more, but fell, insensible with terror, to the earth. When, at length, I came to myself, the tomb was filled with dazzling forms of resplendent beauty; the air rang with music, such as mortals never before heard; and I fled, pursued by my fears, the rest of the soldiers rising and following me, each man fearing to look back, but bewildered we lost our way."

The soldiers hurried forward into the city; while, confirmed now in the certainty that Jesus was risen, I hastened, with Martha and Mary, in the direction of the garden.

"How and where did you behold him, Mary?" I interrogated, as we drew near to the steep path leading to the gate of Joseph's garden.

"When we reached the tomb, with our spices and precious ointments, to embalm the body, we found it open, and the soldiers, who had guarded it, lying about upon the ground like dead men. Upon the stone sat the archangel, but the resplendent light of his apparel and countenance was so tempered to our eyes, that, although we believed it was an angel, we were not terrified, for his looks were serene, and the aspect of his face divinely beautiful, combined with a terrible and indescribable majesty. We shook with fear, and stood still, unable to move, gazing on him in silent expectation.

"'Fear not,' said he in a voice that seemed to fill the air about us with undulating music, 'fear not, daughters of Abraham. I know that ye seek Jesus, which was crucified! He is not here, but is risen, as he foretold. Lo! see the place where the Lord of Life, and Conqueror of Death, hath lain!'

"We then timidly approached, and looked in, and saw the sepulchre empty; but a soft light filled the whole place.

"'Go and tell his disciples that the Lord is risen,' added the angel, 'and that he will go before them into Galilee. There shall they see him not many days hence!'

"When the angel had thus spoken to us," continued Mary, "we departed quickly from the sepulchre with fear and great joy, and ran to go into the city, to bring his disciples word, according to the command of the angel. But I had not advanced so far as the gate of the garden, being behind the rest, when I beheld Jesus himself standing in my path. I stopped, between terror and joy.

"'All hail! daughter of Israel,' he said. 'Be not afraid. I am living, that was dead! Go, Mary, and tell my mother and my brethren, and Peter, and John, and Lazarus, that I am risen, and that I have spoken with you. Be not afraid! I am the resurrection and the life!'

"I then cast myself at his feet, and worshiped him with awe; and when I looked up, he was gone.

"The others did not see him. We now continued on to the city, as if we had wings. But see! we are now at the gate of the garden," added Mary of Bethany, in a low tone of awe. "He must be near us."

But we approached the tomb without seeing any man, having arrived before Peter and John, who had been delayed some time at the Jaffa gate. We, therefore, found no one at the sepulchre. It was open, and empty. The stone in front, on which the archangel sat, was vacant. As we drew near, a bright light suddenly shone out from the tomb; and upon going higher I beheld two angels, clothed in white robes, and with countenances of divine radiance, seated, one at the head and the other at the foot of the slab of marble, on which the body of Jesus had lain.

"Be not afraid, daughters of Jerusalem," said one of the angels, speaking to us in the Hebrew tongue; "He whom ye seek, liveth! He is risen from the tomb, which could not hold him but through his consent; for Jesus is Lord of Life, and Victor over Death and Hell, for evermore! Go your way, and tell his disciples that he awaits them by the seaside."

The angels then vanished from our sight; and at the same moment John and Peter came running, and seeing the stone rolled away, John stooped down, and looked in, and said that he saw the linen clothes in which the body of Jesus had been wrapped, lying folded together, and also the napkin which had been bound about his head. Peter, now coming up, breathless with eagerness and haste, no sooner saw the tomb open, than he went boldly in, and carefully examined all for himself. When we made known to them what the angels had said to us, that Jesus would go before and meet them in Galilee, they rejoiced greatly, and shortly afterwards departed, to hasten into Galilee. I also returned with them, to convey the news to Mary, the mother of Jesus, who had scarcely left her couch, in her great sorrow, since the day of the crucifixion. Mary of Bethany, however, remained, lingering near the tomb, hoping that Jesus had not yet left the garden, and that she might once more behold him.

Seated upon the steps of the tomb, weeping for joy at his resurrection, and wishing once more to behold him, she heard a footstep behind her, and, turning round, saw a man standing near her. It was Jesus himself, and kneeling, she was about to clasp his feet, when he said to her:

"Touch me not, Mary. I am not yet ascended to my Father. But go and tell Lazarus, and my brethren, and my mother, that I ascend ere many days, unto my Father and your Father, and unto my God and your God."

Jesus then vanished out of her sight; and she came and told all these things to us, and to the disciples.

But what pen can describe, my dear father, the amazement and consternation of Caiaphas, and the chief priests, and the rest of his enemies!

Caiaphas, hearing the uproar of the soldiers, sprang from his couch to inquire the cause, and on being assured by his servants that "Jesus had burst his tomb and risen alive from the dead!" he quaked, and became deadly pale.

When Pilate received the account from the centurion of the guard, he said:

"We have crucified a god, as I believed! Henceforth I am accursed!" and leaving his Hall of Judgment, he went and shut himself up in his own room, which he has not since left.

Caiaphas and the chief priests and scribes, in the meanwhile assembled together in full Sanhedrim, and hearing the testimony of the centurion, were convinced that the fact could not be concealed of Jesus' resurrection.

"Who has seen him alive?" demanded the High Priest.

"I have seen him, my lord," answered the centurion. "I saw his pierced feet and hands as he walked past me; and the morning breeze blew aside his mantle and exposed to my eyes the open wound made by the spear of my soldier, Philippus. He was alive, and in full strength of limb!"

"Thou sawest a vision, Roman!" answered Caiaphas. "Come aside with us, and let us talk with thee."

In a few minutes afterwards the centurion left the court of the High Priest's palace, followed by a Gibeonite slave, bearing after him a vase of Persian gold. He has told every one since, that he must have seen a spirit, for "the disciples of Jesus came by night and stole away the body of their master, while they slept, overcome with watching." His soldiers have also been bribed to tell the same tale!

Such is the false version that now goes about the city, my dear father; but there are few that give it credence, even of our enemies. As Æmilius, who is filled with great joy at the resurrection of Jesus, to-day very justly says:

"If these soldiers slept on guard, they merited death therefor, by the military laws of the empire. If, while sleeping, their charge—the dead body of Jesus—was taken away, they deserve death for failing to prevent it. Why then are they not placed under arrest by Pilate's orders, if this story be true? Because Pilate well knows that it is not true! He knows, because he has privately examined many of the soldiers, that Jesus did burst his tomb, and that angels rolled away the stone without breaking his seals, which could not have been left unmarred but by a miracle. He knows that Jesus has arisen—for it is believed that he has also beheld him—at least such is the rumor at the Pretorium. It was the form of Jesus visible before him, doubtless, that drove him in such amazement from his Hall to his secret chamber; for it was remarked that he started, turned deadly pale, and essayed to address the invisible space before him, as if he saw a spirit."

Besides the facts which I have stated, is the increasing testimony of the thousands who, to-day, have gone out of the city to see the sepulchre where He was laid. They say, both enemies of Jesus as well as our friends, that it was impossible for the door to have been opened by any human being, not by Pilate himself, without marring the seals. They also assert that, to remove the stone by night, which would require four men, and to bear forth the body, would have been impossible, if the guard had been present; and if they had been asleep, they must have been awakened with the heavy noise made by rolling the massive door along the hollow pavement outside the sepulchre.

"If," say the common people, "the watch slept, why does not the Procurator put them to death?"

This question remains unanswered, and the watch go about the streets unharmed! My dear father, remember no more my unbelief, but with me believe in Jesus, that he is the Son of God, the Savior of Israel, the immortal Christ of the Prophets.

Your affectionate daughter,

Adina.

LETTER XXXVIII.

Bethany, House of Mary and Martha, a Month after the Passover.

I deeply regret, my dearest father, the delays which have detained you so long from arriving at Jerusalem, but trust that, ere many days, the caravan for which you wait will reach Gaza, and that you will be enabled to resume your journey to the Holy City. I am now at Bethany, where I have been some time making my home.

Uncle Amos has retired, for the present, to his farm, near Jericho, but will be here to-morrow to remain with us. Therefore, when you come near to Jerusalem, instead of going directly into the city, turn aside by the road leading past the king's gardens, and go up the brook of Kedron, into the way to Bethany. I pray that God may preserve you in safety, and soon permit me the happiness of once more embracing you, after three long years of separation.

And what events have transpired in these three years! Once more, my dear father, read carefully over the whole narrative, and answer to yourself this inquiry: Is not this man the Son of God? Is not he the very Christ, the long-looked-for Messias?

Isaias prophesied of the Christ whom he saw afar off, that he should be "a man of sorrows;" that he should be "despised and rejected of men;" that he should be "taken from prison and judgment, and cut off from the land of the living;" that he should be "numbered with the wicked in his death, and make his grave with the rich!" How light, how clear, how plain, all these prophecies now are to me, and to us all! How wonderfully in their minuteness they have been fulfilled, you already know.

His resurrection, also, was foretold by himself, but we did not understand his words until now. When he spoke of destroying the temple, and raising it in three days, he spoke of the tabernacle of his body! Oh, how many sayings, which, when spoken by his sacred lips, we understood not, now rush upon us in all their meaning, proving to us that every step of his life was foreknown to him; that he went forward to his death aware of all things whatsoever that were going to befall him!

But his resurrection was also foretold by the holy David, when he said, "Thou wilt not leave his soul in hell, nor suffer thy Holy One to see corruption;" and his arraignment before Pilate, Caiaphas, and Herod, was foretold by David, when he said: "The kings of the earth set themselves, and the rulers take counsel together, against the Lord, and against his

Anointed;" yet the Lord saith, "Thou art my Son, this day have I begotten thee." Also, my dear father, turn to the Psalms (22) of King David, and compare the following words, which speak of Messias, with what I have described in my previous letters:

"They shoot out the lip at me; they shake the head; they laugh me to scorn. They say, He trusted in the Lord that he would deliver him. Thou hast brought me into the dust of death."

Read the same psalm of the holy king a little farther, and you will see these words, which were put by the royal prophet into the lips of his future Messias:

"The assembly of the wicked have enclosed me. They pierced my hands and my feet. They part my garments among them, and upon my vesture cast lots!"

Read and compare these prophecies of Messias, with the accounts in my letters, dear father, and you will not only be convinced that Jesus is the Messias, but you will perceive that his humiliation and sufferings before Pilate and Caiaphas, his agony on the cross, his death and burial, instead, as we ignorantly conceived, of being evidences that he was not the Christ, are proof that he was the very Son of the Highest—the Shiloh of Jehovah foretold by the prophets—the Anointed King of Israel.

Oh, wonderful is all this! How marvelous these things passing before our eyes! Now all is dazzlingly clear! The Prophets are unveiled to our sight, and we see that these things must have happened to him. Oh, our darkness, our blindness, to have seen in the prophecies of Messias only the passages which speak of his glory and power! Read the Prophets no longer, my dearest father, with a veil before your eyes! See, in all you read, Jesus as the end of the Prophets, the goal of all their far-seeing prophecies, the veritable and sure realization of their prophetic visions.

Thus, my dear father, has Jesus in all particulars proved himself to be the subject of all prophecy—the King of Israel. But you will now ask, "Is he to re-establish the throne of David, and live forever?"

Yes, but not a Jerusalem of earthly splendor. Oh, how clear are all things to my apprehension now! The Jerusalem in which his throne is to be placed, is heavenly, and the true Jerusalem, of which the present one is but the material type—what the body is to the soul of man.

Jesus has talked with me since his resurrection, and explained all this to me, and much more that is wonderful and full of joy.

It is now four weeks since he arose, and in that time he has been not only seen by all the disciples, but by hundreds of his followers. The only change in his usual appearance, dear father, to the eye, is a transparent paleness, which gives a soft radiance to his whole aspect, and a certain majestic reserve, which awes all who draw near to him; so that men speak in his presence in subdued whispers. His mother, happiest of women now, as she was before the most wretched, ever sits at his feet, and silently enjoys his sacred presence, seldom speaking, and looking up to him rather as a worshiper to her God, than a mother upon her son. That he is in the flesh in reality, and not a spirit, he has proven to his disciples, by eating with them; and in a remarkable way to an incredulous disciple, called Thomas, who, not believing that Jesus was risen in his real body from the dead, was told by the divine Lord to place his fingers into his hands, and his hand into his side; which Thomas, convinced, with awe refused to do; but, falling at his feet in amazement and adoration, worshiped him as God.

To-day his disciples are with him in the gardens of David, at Bethlehem, where he is holding daily a solemn council with the eleven, unfolding to them the glory of his kingdom, and opening their understandings to the clear apprehension of all which the prophets have written concerning him. John, who is a member of this divine council, says that the power of Jesus, the extent and majesty of his kingdom, the infinite results of his death and resurrection, are not to be conceived of by those who have not listened to these sublime revelations of his own lips.

"He hath shown us," said John, "how that his true office as Son of God, and Son of Man, is to be a mediator. He showed us that he himself was the High Priest, and how that the cross was the veritable altar of this great world's sacrifice, and its Temple the whole earth and heavens!"

How wonderful, dear father, is all this! He further teaches his disciples that he will shortly ascend from the earth, to enter upon his celestial reign, and that his subjects there are to be all who love him and keep his commandments. It is to be a kingdom of holiness, and none will enter there but the pure in heart. He says, further, that as we do now confess our sins over the blood of the victim we sacrifice for ourselves in the Temple, so henceforth we must look to him (by faith when we shall see him no longer), slain a sacrifice for us, and confess our sins to the Father for his sake. Jesus has moreover taught his disciples that the Gentiles are to share equally with the children of Abraham the benefits of his death and resurrection; that this good news shall be proclaimed to them by his disciples, and that they will gladly hear it and believe.

"The fountain of my everlasting kingdom," saith he, "truly shall be laid upon earth in the hearts of men; but the building is with God, eternal in the heavens. The tomb through which I have passed is its gate, and all who would come after me, and enter in, must follow in my footsteps."

Thomas then asked his Lord whither he would go, and the way; how he would leave the earth, since he could die no more.

"Thou shalt see for thyself ere many days pass," answered Jesus. "In that I have risen, all whom my Father giveth me shall rise also from the dead; and those whom I raise up, I will take with me the way I go; for where I am, they shall evermore be with me also."

Such, dear father, is a brief account of what John has told us, touching the divine teaching of Messias, the Son of God, respecting his kingdom. Yet much is still mysterious; but we know enough to be willing to trust ourselves to him for this life, and for that which is to come. We know that all power is given into his hands, and that he can save all men who believe in and accept him.

What is remarkable, dear father, notwithstanding the Jews have heard that Jesus walks everywhere through Jewry, yet no efforts are made to lay hands on him. At his presence, crowds of his enemies fly like the stricken multitude before the advancing sirocco. His presence in Judea is a present dread, like some great evil, to those who fear him; but like a celestial blessing to more who love him. Pilate, on the eve of making a journey last week to Bethel, before quitting the city dispatched couriers in advance to ascertain "whether Jesus the Crucified was on the line of his route!" Caiaphas, having occasion to go to Jericho, a few days after the Passover, hearing that Jesus had been seen with his disciples on the road, made a circuit round by Luz and Shiloh, in order not to meet him. The gates of the city are kept constantly shut, lest he should enter within the walls; some of the chief priests fearing greatly to behold his face, while others imagine that he is engaged in raising an army, to advance upon and take Jerusalem from the Romans.

I rejoice to see by your last letter, that you may be expected to reach here the week after next. Oh that you were here now, that you might be taken by John to see Jesus! for from what he says he will not long remain visible among us. Whither he goeth or how he goeth away, no man can say.

Faithfully, your loving daughter,

Adina.

LETTER XXXIX.

Bethany, Forty Days after the Resurrection.

My Dearest Father:

With emotions that nearly deprive me of the power to hold my pen, and with trembling fingers that make the words I write almost illegible, I sit down to make known to you the extraordinary event which will mark this day in all future time as the most worthy to be noted among men.

On the fortieth day after the resurrection, my dear father, early in the morning, Jesus left the house of Mary and Lazarus, where he had sat up with us all night speaking to us of the glories of the life above, and the excellency of heart and purity of life required of all who should enter it.

"Lord," said Martha, as he went forth, "whither goest thou?"

"Come and see," he answered. "Whither I go ye shall know, and the way ye shall know: for where I am ye shall also be, and all those who believe in me."

"Lord," said Mary, kneeling at his feet, "return at noon, and remain with us during the heat of the day."

"Mary," said Jesus, laying his hand gently upon her forehead, "I am going to my Father's house! There thou shalt dwell with me in mansions not made with hands."

Thus speaking, he walked slowly onward towards the hill of Bethany, not far from the place where Lazarus was buried. He was followed not only by Mary, Martha, Lazarus, and John, my Cousin Mary, and myself, but by all the disciples. There were at least five hundred persons in all, moving on with him ere he reached the green hillside beyond the village; for all followed him, expecting to hear more glorious revelations from his lips.

"He goes to the hill to pray," said one of his disciples.

"Nay, he goeth to show us some mighty miracle, from the expression of power and majesty in his aspect," said Thomas to me, gazing upon the Lord with awe; for each moment as he ascended the hill, his countenance grew more glorious with a certain God-like majesty, and shone as the face of Moses descending from Mount Sinai. We all hung back with adoring awe, and alone he proceeded onward, a wide space being left by us between ourselves and him. Yet there was no terror in the glory which surrounded and shined out from him, but rather a holy radiance, that seemed to be the very light of holiness and peace.

"So looked he," said John to us, "when we beheld him transfigured in the mount with Elias and Moses."

The hill, which is not lofty, was soon surmounted by his sacred feet. He stood upon its apex alone. We kept back near the brow of the hill, for his raiment shone now like the sun, while his countenance was as lightning. We shaded our eyes to behold him. All was now expectation, and a looking for some mighty event—what, we knew not! John drew nearest to him, and upon his knees, with clasped hands, looked towards him earnestly; for he knew, as he afterwards told us, what would take place. Joy and yet tears were on his face, as he gazed with blinded eyes, as one gazes on the noonday sun, upon his divine Master. It was a scene, dear father, impressive beyond expression. Jesus seemed for a moment to survey the scenes of his sufferings, of his ignominy and death, with the look of a divine conqueror. He then turned to his disciples and said:

"Ye have been with me in my sorrows, and you shall now begin to behold my glory. Remember all things which I have taught you concerning my kingdom. Go forth and teach the glad tidings of salvation to all men, and baptize all nations in the name of the Father, and of the Son, and of the Holy Ghost; and lo, I am with you alway, even unto the end of the world."

Thus speaking, in a voice that thrilled every bosom with emotions indescribable, he extended his hands above their heads and blessed them, while we all fell upon our faces to the ground also, to receive his blessing.

He then lifted up his eyes to the calm blue depths of heaven, and said in the same words he had spoken on the night of the Passover, as John had told me:

"And now, O Father, glorify thou me with thine own self, with the glory which I had with thee before the world was!"

As he spoke, we raised our faces from the ground, to behold him leaving the earth, rising from the hilltop into the air, with a slow and majestic ascension, his hands outspread over us who were beneath, as if shedding down blessings upon us all. The loud burst of surprise which rose from five hundred voices at seeing him soar away into the atmosphere, was followed by a profound and awful silence, as we watched him rise and still rise, ascending and still ascending, into the upper air, his whole form growing brighter and brighter, as the distance widened between his feet and the earth!

Upon our knees, in speechless wonder, we followed his ascent with our amazed eyes, not a word being spoken by any soul; nay, hearts might have been heard beating in the intense expectation of the moment!

Lo! in the far-off height of heaven, we beheld suddenly appear a bright cloud, no larger than a man's hand, but each instant it expanded and grew broader and brighter, and, swift as the winged lightning, descended through the firmament downward, until we beheld it evolve itself into a glittering host of angels, which no man could number, countless as the stars of heaven. As these shining legions descended, they parted into two bands, and sweeping along the air, met the ascending Son of God in mid-sky! The rushing of their ten thousand times ten thousand wings, was heard as the sound of many waters. Surrounding Jesus, like a shining cloud, they received him into their midst, and hid him from our eyes amid the glories of their celestial splendor!

Now came to our ears the sounds of heavenly song, a sublimer chorus than earth ever heard before. From the squadrons of Seraphim and Cherubim encircling with their linked wings the Son of God, came, like the unearthly music one hears in the dreams of night, these words, receding, as they mounted upward with the Conqueror of Death and Hell:

"Lift up your heads, O ye gates!And be ye lifted up, ye everlasting doors;And the King of Glory shall come in!"

This chorus seemed to be answered from the inmost heavens, as if an archangel were standing at its portals, keeping watchful guard over the entrance facing the earth.

"Who is the King of Glory?"

"The Lord strong and mighty, even the Lord mighty in battle against principalities and powers,"

was chanted back from the ascending escort of Jesus, in the sublimest strains of triumphant joy.

"Lift up your heads, O ye gates! and be ye lifted up, ye everlasting doors, and the King of Glory shall come in!"

Upon this we heard a mighty voice, as it were in heaven, accompanied by the sound of a trumpet, and ten thousand voices about the throne of Jehovah seemed to say:

"God is coming up with a shout. He rideth upon the heavens! He ascendeth on high! He hath led captivity captive, and received gifts for men. O clap your hands, all ye people of earth! Shout his triumph, ye hosts of heaven!

"Fling wide your gates, O City of God! Be ye lifted up, ye everlasting doors, for the King of Glory enters in!"

Ascending and still ascending, receding and still receding, fainter and fainter, came down to earth the angelic choruses, when at length the brightest cloud of angels faded away into the upper heaven, the Son of God shining in their midst, like a central sun, surrounded by a luminous halo; till finally, like a star, they remained a few moments longer, and then the heavens received him out of our sight.

While we stood gazing up into the far skies, hoping, expecting, yet doubting if we should ever behold him again, two bright stars seemed to be descending from the height of heaven above us. In a few seconds we saw that they were angels. Alighting on the place where Jesus had left, they said to the eleven, "Why gaze ye up into heaven, ye men of Galilee? This same Jesus, whom ye have seen go into heaven, shall so come in like manner as ye have now seen him ascend!" Thus speaking, they vanished out of our sight!

Such, my dear father, is the appropriate crowning event of the extraordinary life of Jesus, both Lord and Christ!

His kingdom is, therefore, my dear father, clearly not of this world, as he said to Pilate, the Procurator; but it is Above.

Doubt, then, no longer, dearest father! Jesus, the Son of Mary in his human nature, was the Son of God in his divine nature; an incomprehensible and mysterious union, whereby he had brought together in harmony the two natures, separated far apart by sin, by giving his own body as an offering, to reconcile both in one immaculate body upon the cross. There is now no more condemnation to them who believe in him and accept him.

But I cannot write all I would say to you, dearest father. When we meet— which you rejoice me in saying, will be on the first day of the week, at Jerusalem—I will unfold to you all that the divine and glorified Jesus has taught me. Doubt not that he is Messias. Hesitate not to accept him; for he is the end of Moses, and of the Law, and of the Prophets, the very Shiloh who should come and restore all things; to whom be glory, power, dominion, majesty, and excellency, evermore.

Your loving daughter,

Adina.

THE END.